Dr. Dave's Cyberhood

● ● ● ● ● ● ● ● ● ● ● ● ●

Making Media Choices That Create a Healthy Electronic Environment for Your Kids

David Walsh, Ph.D.

with

Kristin Parker and Monica Walsh

A FIRESIDE BOOK
Published by Simon & Schuster
NEW YORK   LONDON   TORONTO   SYDNEY   SINGAPORE

 **FIRESIDE**
Rockefeller Center
1230 Avenue of the Americas
New York, NY 10020

Designed by Christine Weathersbee

Manufactured in the United States of America

10   9   8   7   6   5   4   3   2   1

Library of Congress Cataloging-in-Publication Data
Walsh, David Allen.
    Dr. Dave's cyberhood : making media choices that create a healthy
electronic environment for your kids / David Walsh with Kristin Parker and
Monica Walsh.
        p.   cm.
    "A Fireside book."
    Includes index.
    1. Mass media and children.   I. Title: Doctor Dave's cyberhood.
II. Parker, Kristin.   III. Walsh, Monica.   IV. Title.
P94.5.C55 W35 2001
305.23—dc21   00-067131

ISBN 0-7432-0573-1

Contents

• • • • • • • • • •

Acknowledgments

Dr. Dave's Cyberhood is the product of collaboration involving many people that I would like to thank and acknowledge. First, I want to express my appreciation to the thousands of parents and teachers who have attended my workshops. Their questions, suggestions, and insights appear throughout this book. I am indebted to the staff of the National Institute on Media and the Family for their constant support, inspiration, and patience: Beth Zeilinger, Eileen McCarthy Harness, Doug Gentile, Marilyn VanOverbeke, Gwen Aaberg, Laura Torgerud, and LaDonna Seely Coudron. I also want to acknowledge the support and encouragement provided by Fairview Health Services in Minneapolis, especially to Fairview's president, David Page, and to Vice President Barbara Nye. The National Institute on Media and the Family exists because Fairview Health Services believes in the importance of our mission.

I would also especially like to thank those whose support along the way has been invaluable: Target Corporation and its leaders, especially Gail Dorn, Ann Aronson, John Pellegrene, and Jean Knutson; Don and Jane Brattain for their commitment to children; the McKnight Foundation; the Minneapolis Foundation; the Robins, Kaplan, Miller and Ciresi Foundation; and the Graco Foundation.

There are also several individuals whose advice and support have been invaluable: Susan Eilertsen, professional advisor and friend; my agent, Mark Sottnick; and my Fireside editor, Lisa Considine.

Most of all, I want to thank my two collaborators. Although

I must assume responsibility for the ideas you are about to read, these two women helped me bring them to life in this book. Kristin Parker is the gifted writer who was able to transform my prose into a form that I hope you will understand and enjoy. Monica Walsh is the natural teacher behind all the tools woven throughout this book. Not only do I salute their talent, I also thank them for their patience and hard work. Most of all, I admire them for their commitment to children and their respect for parents.

David Walsh, Ph.D.
Minneapolis

Preface

We live in exciting and changing times. The signs are all around us—kids carrying pagers, computers in the classroom, video screens in public rest rooms, TV channels multiplying like weeds, virtual-reality games, and personalized web pages. Just a couple of years ago, the term *media* brought movies and TV programs to mind. Now a listing of the different media forms could fill the rest of this page.

The pace of change won't be slowing down any time soon either. In fact, it will be picking up. Children growing up today, the Internet generation, take the new media for granted. They're a part of everyday life. They are wired to the world and to each other unlike any generation before them.

Just as generations of kids before them were comfortable running and biking around the neighborhood they lived in, so this Internet generation is comfortable linking with people and places all over the world via the click of a mouse. Their neighborhood is the world they can access, visit, and hang out in through electronic connections—their *Cyberhood*.

Most of us parents marvel at these changes. We are amazed each time the pace of change picks up. We get excited about the possibilities for our children. We may also be alarmed about the possible dangers. How do we help our children find their way around the virtually connected world so that they are reaping the benefits while avoiding the pitfalls? That's the challenge for us all.

I hope this book will help to map out a path through the maze of choices. It provides two things: information and tools. The *information* will provide the knowledge about where media are and where they are going. It will also provide some principles to guide parental decision making. The *tools* are the exercises, questionnaires, and planning guides that will help you incorporate this information into your lives. Having information is good. Translating that information into action is even better. That's the goal of this book.

Dr.
Dave's
Cyberhood

CHAPTER ONE

· · · · · · · · · · ·

Parenting in the Media Age

Children are the purpose of life.
We were once children and someone took
care of us. Now it is our turn to care.

———Cree Indian Elder

This quote has long been a favorite of mine, so centered and wise, so accepting of what parenthood is all about: making children the priority. All children deserve to come first, from rural towns and pulsing metros, living with two caregivers and one, economically secure and disadvantaged. As parents, our basic job is to care for our children: to see to their physical, emotional, social, and spiritual needs. Like you, the overwhelming majority of parents *want* to take good care of their children. It is with this belief that this book unfolds.

Just how you go about caring for your child depends on your individual family situation. If you live in the country, for example, keeping your child safe requires certain considerations, while living in a city neighborhood requires others. Or, if you work in an office full time, managing your child's care after school is different than if you work at home.

Whatever the mix of variables is, one factor that figures into the equation for all parents is the society in which they are raising their children. History has shown, many times over, how spectacular events reshape the world, changing the way people live, work, and communicate. Consider the invention of the printing press in the mid-fifteenth century. The implications were astounding. For the first time, printed information became widely available, the ability to read spread across generations, and literacy took root in civilization. The significance of this event goes much deeper: the ability to read and write transformed the way we think, in effect, ending the Dark Ages and beginning the Renaissance.

Whether you realize it, you exercise this transformation every time you move from spoken to written language. Just think about how your vocabulary expands when you write. You take the time to choose the words that most precisely, powerfully, or effectively capture what you want to communicate. When you speak, you have to the pull the words out quickly to keep a sentence going. Written language also brings discipline to the thought process. When you write, you have to organize your thinking differently from when you speak; writing is not just a stream of consciousness. You have to systemize your thoughts into outlines, paragraphs, and chapters. When you look at the whole picture, that one event—the invention of the printing press—is pretty impressive.

New York University professor Neil Postman adds yet another chapter to the legacy of the printing press. He argues that its invention led to the actual concept of *childhood*—the notion that children go through stages of development to become adults. Prior to the availability of the printed word, children were thought of as a minature adults or little people. This perspective began to change with the realization that learning to read and write does not happen overnight; that children learn and develop this skill over a period of years. The idea of childhood as a time of development began to take shape. Coming from our contemporary perspective, where there is so much focus on issues of child development, it's hard to imagine there was a time when being a child simply meant being a little person.

Another history-making, culture-shaking event took place in the early nineteenth century: the Industrial Revolution. We consider it significant because it gave rise to mass production. Goods that were made more efficiently, in greater quantities, and of higher quality, meant a higher standard of living. The effect of this event on family culture was just as remarkable. Prior to the revolution, the worlds of work and family life were interwoven, the line separating them indistinct. If you were a candlemaker or a shoemaker, your shop was at the front of the house and your family lived at the back. If you were a farmer, your fields surrounded your cottage. As soon as the kids were old enough, they took part in the family business. Parents and children interacted all day long. Children learned skills right along with attitudes and values in this natural blend of family life and work.

When the Industrial Revolution took hold, manufacturing centers appeared, cities grew up around them, and people began to migrate from rural livelihoods to urban employment. In the process, family life changed dramatically. With adults off to factories every day, parents not only interacted with their children less, they had to make arrangements for the care of the young ones while they were at work. Widespread public education was the eventual outcome. The way kids learned skills, attitudes, and values took a critical turn.

This history minilesson helps put us in the right frame of mind to look at our own situation. Families are now in the midst of a revolution at least as profound as these historical milestones. And it, too, is changing the way children—our children—are being raised. Some call it the *Dawn of the Information Age,* others the *Digital Revolution,* or the *Telecommu-*

nications Revolution. By any name, it is changing the way we live and communicate at a faster rate than any other force. Its dazzling array of electronic media has become essential to our lives. In fact, our kids spend more time with these media than doing any other activity in their waking hours. Inevitably, this changes what it means to care for our children.

Because this incredible revolution is becoming our way of life we may not appreciate just how awesome it is, but you don't have to look far for evidence. You may have seen the Hallmark card that lets you record a greeting. For about $8.95, the recipient of your good wishes can hear the words right out of your mouth via a tiny computer chip imbedded in the card. That you can buy a card that speaks for you is novel enough but, what's really stunning, is that there is more computing power in that one chip than existed in the entire world prior to 1950. Perhaps even more remarkable is the electronic picture frame: You give it to a loved one; then send digital images via e-mail directly to the frame. Grandma and Grandpa can have a new picture of their grandchild every day.

Here's another perspective on the Digital Revolution: If the speed of change in the computer industry over the last fifty years was matched in the auto industry, we would be buying our new cars for one-tenth of one penny. Those inexpensive cars would be traveling at the speed of light.

To further prove the point, if you buy a computer today, you have to resign yourself to Moore's Law (after Gordon Moore, founder of Intel, the leading manufacturer of microprocessors). It promises that "the speed and capacity of the microprocessor doubles every eighteen months." So, your new PC is becoming outdated before the carton even makes it to the recycler.

This digital age has even changed our language. We have a whole vocabulary for talking about how much information can be digitally stored. The first computers held kilobytes of information (mere thousands of bytes), only to be replaced by megabytes (millions of bytes), then gigabytes (billions of bytes), soon terabytes (trillions of bytes), and, eventually, petabytes (quadrillions of bytes).

The same thing has happened to measuring time. Look at any athletic scoreboard. Instead of hours, minutes, and seconds, we break down the last moments of the game into hundredths of a second. If that doesn't do it, we can measure in milliseconds. In this digital world, we can measure increments of time in nanoseconds, and, even finer yet, in picoseconds.

This gives us a feel for the scope of the revolution we are in. We're as much a part of it as it's a part of us. Technology that didn't exist a few years ago is so ingrained in our daily living that we hardly give it a second thought. We keep inventing and incorporating more and more tools to help us communicate and receive information. Voice mail, e-mail, pagers, cell phones, CDs, video games, TV, the Internet—a reverberating explosion of media, a *media age*. These everyday wonders have transformed how we do our work, how we communicate with each other, how we entertain ourselves. We're on a roll and not slowing down.

This is the world in which our children are growing up. This is the world in which we have to care for them. It is an amazing world, to be sure, and the benefits of a media age are real—the ability to instantly communicate with millions of people simultaneously is but one of the marvels. What should be important to us, as parents and caregivers, however, is not whether we should label media as good or bad: They are neither, entirely. What matters is that we recognize media for what they are above all else: powerful. And they are available to our children every day.

By 2003, major companies hope to cover the earth with wireless phone and data networks, launching nearly 1,000 telecom satellites. (*America Unwired,* Harris Corporation, 1998.)

A thirty-second AT&T commercial succinctly illustrates our media-saturated world. The spot opens with a grade-school girl and her friends huddled over lunch in the cafeteria. The friends plead with her to reveal the name of her new crush. Finally, amidst pledges of secrecy, she gives in. The next thing you know, the news is out via the technological grapevine. We see kids sending faxes, getting e-mail, talking on cell phones, and so on, until the girl arrives home only to find out that her mother already knows, and worse yet, the crush, Bobby, is waiting for her in the family room. I'm sure the intent of the commercial wasn't to horrify parents at the power of media unleashed in the hands of children, nor to mirror how quickly they are growing up because of them. However, it does reflect the pervasiveness of media and just how much they have changed the way we live and communicate.

For parents, media has changed something else: how we define caring for our children. Consider this for a moment: You might agree that taking care of your child means knowing where he or she is, because there are potential dangers and influences you want to keep at bay. So, you know where in the neighborhood your child is playing. Living in the Media Age changes even this basic notion. Now, your child can wander through the infinite spaces of cyber neighborhoods, via the Internet, while sitting in her bedroom. And, just as there are real places you wouldn't want your child to spend time in, there are plenty of inappropriate cyberhoods he or she shouldn't be visiting either.

• • • • • • • •

Seventy-three percent of children ages ten to seventeen use the Internet or e-mail at home. (*National Public Radio/Kaiser/Kennedy Technology Study,* 2000.)

• • • • • • • •

Here's another angle on the reality of parenthood. You wouldn't dream of letting your child subsist on an ice cream diet—no matter how much she would like it—because it isn't good for her. You know how important balanced nutrition is to her physical health and development. Yet, with the accessibility of television today, many children are allowed to consume a steady diet of programming (and the advertising that comes with it), unchecked and unmonitored. Common sense tells you there's a question of *emotional* health and development at stake here. Later on in this book, you'll get a good look at this issue as well as at the risks associated with other forms of media.

As parents and caregivers, our basic role is still the same—to care for our children—but, what that caring entails has changed, because of the society in which we live. So, we need to adapt our caregiving to fit the circumstances. Just as you see a family trip to the lake as an opportunity for fun, you also recognize the power of open water and know that it is your responsibility to look out for your children and ensure their well-being. You adapt your caregiving to fit the circumstances. Caring for your child in this age of electronic media is

Television watching is the top after-school activity chosen by children ages six to seventeen. (*Center for Media Education,* 1997.)

no different. You feel a responsibility to guide and protect them—to care for them—to the best of your abilities.

Which brings us to the issue of time, because caring for your child requires your time. You know this well. That one word—*time*—can make your heart beat a little faster and your shoulders start to inch up. Not because you don't care enough to spend the time, but because you *care so much,* and you have to work so hard to get more mileage out of a finite day and measurable resources. And now, on top of everything else you have to care about, you have to manage your children's media diet, too.

All the technology we have at our fingertips is supposed to alleviate the crunch but, ironically, it intensifies the problem. It promises us more time to do the things we want (remember talk of the thirty-hour work week?). Instead, the pace of everything has sped up, and we keep trying to fit more and more into the time that's available. As technology enables things to work faster and faster, we expect shorter and shorter turn-arounds. When we get an e-mail, the expectation is an imme-diate response. So, instead of more time, we actually end up with less.

It's no wonder we're primed for the temptation of media: that they will entertain and occupy our kids. With time obliga-tions piling up, it's very easy to turn to those captivating elec-tronic baby-sitters—television, video games, and computers. At the end of a long day, it's far easier to hand off responsibil-ity to technology, far easier not to put out.

The problem is, while we care about raising healthy, happy, well-adjusted, children with healthy attitudes and values, electronic media do not share the same objectives. Electronic media are interested in only one thing: making money. Elec-tronic media are interested in our children as consumers, not learners, as you'll see later on. Our kids are going to be raised either by us, or by electronic media.

A finding that appeared in the October 1998 Nielsen Rat-ings is very telling. A poll of family viewing habits revealed that the television show most watched by two- to five-year-olds was *Friends*. Of course, children this young were not choosing to watch *Friends*. They watched because their parents turned it on. The show airs in early prime time, when many children are not yet in bed. However, since we can't expect the media to change to meet our individual needs for the sake of our chil-dren, we have to make changes ourselves. We have to take an-other look—a critical look—at the media we've become so accustomed to.

You can give it a try right now. Imagine that someone you know and feel comfortable with has just rung your doorbell and asked to come in and talk to your children. You invite her into the family room and gather up the kids. Your guest then proceeds to persuade your children to accept certain values by exhorting, cajoling, and mesmerizing them. The method is offensive enough but what's worse is that you disagree with the values being sold. What do you do? Allow this guest to stay, or put your foot down and show her the door?

You and every family in America has a live-in guest like this to contend with every day: television. However, it's much more persuasive and slick than anyone who might ring the doorbell. And, we're *so* comfortable with it. It's a regular part of our lives. We're so used to the images and sounds TV feeds our eyes and ears that often we don't register the messages, or their impact. When it comes to our children, we *have* to pay attention, because *they* are. We have to make decisions about what is appropriate for our children to experience. We have to put the same thought into these decisions that we would into where they play, what food they eat, and who we hire to babysit them. And this takes our time.

> Three out of five teenagers have a TV set in their bedroom. (*Media in the Home, 2000*, Annenberg Public Policy Center, 2000.)

If you feel your heart racing again, remind yourself of what you already know: that your child is your priority. You know it, you feel it, you believe it. Reminding yourself of this is what fuels you and keeps you on track in the midst of a million things competing for your time. It's what allows you to take a breath when things are at their craziest, and let go a little when everything else doesn't get done so perfectly. In the face of this clarity, time doesn't control you. It becomes yours again, instead of a commodity controlled by the momentum of a hurry-up world. And when it is yours to give your child, you have something media can't give them.

Learning what it means to care for your child in an age of electronic media is not only the job of parenthood today, it is preparation for what's to come. The media landscape we live in is constantly evolving. Even five years from now, the technology we will have at our disposal will be very different. The lines separating media will dissolve: One remote will move us instantly from one medium to another. Interactive TV will filter into households everywhere. The benefits will be greater, and so will be the potential dangers. As a parent, you will need to keep pace and adapt as the definition of a caring parent evolves.

Now that you are beginning to realize what it means to be a parent in the Media Age, you can get on with it. Take a good look at the media your child is using, exploring, and experiencing. You can understand what makes it so powerful. You can learn how to care for your child in the Media Age, then start doing it. This book is dedicated to helping you make the changes and be more in charge. It will reinforce your belief that you can do something about how your child is growing up. It will rekindle your hope. From beginning to end, it supports you in your pursuit of what matters most—your kids.

Your Cyberhood Map

When we travel into unfamiliar territory, a good map helps us find our way. Since we will be the ones guiding our children as the Digital Revolution unfolds, it would be nice to have a map through the new and changing cyberhoods, the worlds of electronic media. Each chapter in this book will help you map the boundaries and terrain within those worlds. Along the way you'll identify *cyberhoods*—websites, virtual game spaces, learning environments—you feel confident letting your children explore. There are others you'll want to avoid. No one but you can identify which is which. There are just too many variables. Each of our children is different, and each of us has our own perspective on which values are most important.

The activities that are included in every chapter are intended to help locate appropriate cyberhoods for your family. Each activity focuses on one of five different thematic categories.

 *Types of media* our family uses or will use.

 Media smarts describe how media works.

 Values that our family holds important.

 Time our children spend on different activities.

 What *action steps* we want to choose to manage media in our families.

You'll see one of these icons alongside each activity.

CHAPTER ONE ACTIVITIES

The goal of this book is to develop healthy media habits. The activities in chapters 1 and 2 will help focus attention on just what kinds of media affect us every day. All these media teach our children values. Comparing our family values and media values is an important step in constructing your map. The Media Measure activity is a valuable tool for you to measure not only what media is used, but also how it is used in your home.

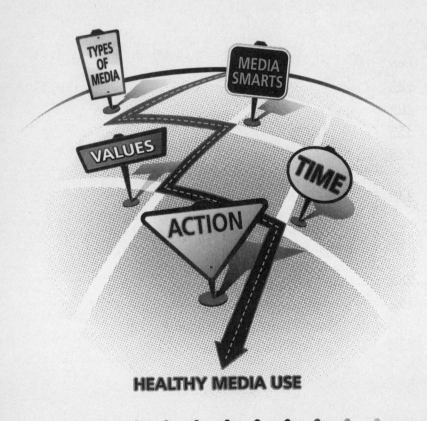

Activity: Who's Plugged In?

For parents or parents and children ages ten and up.

Test your intuition. Guess how many families, kids, and so on, own or use various types of media. Match a percentage from the first column with a type of media in the second column. Circle what you consider to be the five most common items. Compare your answers with the answers on the next page and see if there are any surprises.

Percent (%)

98%	_____	American families with television sets
70%	_____	American families with radios
35%	_____	American families with VCRs
82%	_____	American kids with TVs in their bedrooms
43%	_____	American youth with their own stereo equipment
47%	_____	American teens with their own CD/cassette player
98%	_____	American families with computers
78%	_____	American households with home access to the Internet
57%	_____	American families with video-game equipment
8%	_____	American families with faxes

69% _____ American households with telephones

22% _____ American families with answering machines/voice mail

53% _____ American teens with pagers

14% _____ American adults with cell phones

94% _____ American teens with own cell phones

99% _____ American families who subscribe to cable or satellite TV

ANSWERS

99% American families with television sets[1]

98% American families with radios[2]

98% American families with VCRs[3]

53% American kids with TV in their bedroom[4]

35% American teens with their own stereo equipment[5]

57% American teens with their own CD or cassette player[6]

69% American households with computers[7]

[1]Nielsen, *Media Research*, 1995.
[2]"The Silent Boom," *Forbes,* July 7, 1997, p. 170.
[3]"Media in the Home 1999: "The Fourth Annual Survey of Parents and Children," The Annenberg Public Policy Center, 1999.
[4]"Kids and Media @ The New Millenium," Kaiser Family Foundation, November, 1999.
[5]1998 Roper Youth Report.
[6]*Ibid.*
[7]Kaiser Family Foundation.

43%	American households with home access to the Internet[8]
70%	American families with video-game equipment[9]
22%	American families with faxes[10]
94%	American households with telephones[11]
82%	American families with answering machines/voice mail[12]
14%	American teens with pagers[13]
57%	American adults with cell phones[14]
8%	American teens with own cell phones[15]
78%	American households who subscribe to cable or satellite TV[16]

We Americans use a lot of media. We can hardly imagine life without TVs, computers, radios, and, now, cell phones and other wireless communication. Our children will live in an even more media-saturated world. We parents can help maximize the benefits of these media by developing healthy family media habits.

[8]"Never Lonelier Crowd Emerges in Internet Study," *New York Times*, February 16, 2000, p. A1.
[9]Kaiser Family Foundation.
[10]NPR/Kaiser/Kennedy School Technology Survey," National Public Radio, 2000.
[11]FCC, "Telephone Subscribership Report," January 26, 1998.
[12]NPR/Kaiser/Kennedy.
[13]Reed, Hundt. *America Unwired* (Melbourne, FL: Harris Corporation, 1998).
[14]NPR/Kaiser/Kennedy School.
[15]*Ibid.*
[16]*Ibid.*

Activity: The Digital Revolution

For parents (with help from kids ages ten and up).

In the last one hundred years, we've gone from books and letters to telephone to radio to television to computers and wireless communication. Do you know some of the new language of the digital revolution? Here are some terms. See how many you can match.

1. Terabyte   A. A small program that can cause your hard drive to crash. Contracted by downloading infected files or trading floppy disks.

2. HDTV   B. A service that connects your TV to the Internet via a phone line.

3. E-mail   C. A lot of memory for your computer.

4. CD-ROM   D. Interactive games played online between players from different parts of the world.

5. Cookie   E. Electronic messages sent from one Internet server to another, posted to a user's address.

6. Online Gaming   F. Junk e-mail messages.

7. Virus   G. A plastic disk that can hold 650 megabytes of memory.

8. SPAM

H. Computer language that is used to add animation, sound and interactive features to Web pages.

9. Java

I. A small file placed on your computer when you enter a website. This program tracks every click of your mouse at that site.

10. WebTV

J. Pictures and sound sent in digital format, delivers a program with movielike quality.

Answers: 1. C 2. J 3. E 4. G 5. I 6. D 7. A 8. F 9. H 10. B

Activity: Media Map

For parents and children ages four through ten.

Part of taking charge of electronic media is knowing just what it is, where it is, and who's using it.

Make a media map. Label a box for each room in your house. Use additional sheets of paper if necessary. Draw in the different types of media (TVs, radios, computers, etc.) in that room. Write the names of the users next to each type of media. For example:

Mary

Living Room		TV/ VCR	Mom
			Elly
			Mary
Computer	Stereo		Brian

Dan, Erin

Do this for each room in your home. Don't forget that radio in the bathroom or that telephone in the bedroom. (Hint: You may want to use a larger piece of paper for this activity if children are involved.)

If you have a young child, you may want to play a game of Tag the Media. In a given room, ask the child to find the things that help us communicate, talk to, or get ideas from other people. Label it (i.e., TV) with a sticky note, and list users below. Have the child stick the note on the medium.

Activity: Media Diet

For parents.

As parents, we choose foods for our children that will help their bodies grow strong and healthy. Likewise, we must also try to choose media that will help their minds and spirits grow healthy and strong.

In each column, list what you want healthy foods and healthy media to do for your child.

HEALTHY BODY Food Diet	HEALTHY MIND AND SPIRIT Media Diet
Strengthen bones and muscles	Encourage curious thinkers
Promote an active lifestyle	Promote altruistic role models
_____	_____
_____	_____
_____	_____

● ● ● ● ● ● ● ● ● ●

_____   _____

_____   _____

List what you want   List what you want
healthy foods to do   healthy media to do
for your child   for your child

Activity: Media Measure

For parents.

This inventory will help you take a quick measure not only of the kinds of media your family uses, but how media are used in your home.

At the start of each media category you will see three traffic signs, which will help you evaluate your answers.

Go   **Caution**   **Stop**

For each kind of media that your family uses, circle the answers that describe your family's media habits. In each column, Y stands for Yes; S, sometimes; N, no.

TELEVISION
Think about your family's television viewing habits.

	Go	Caution	Stop
Does your child have a television in her/his room?	N	S	Y

● ● ● ● ● ● ● ● ● ●

Does your child watch more than one to two hours of television per day?	N	S	Y
Do you have rules about when TV can be watched? (Not before school, not until homework is done, etc.)	Y	S	N
Do you have TV on during meals?	N	S	Y
Do you monitor your child's viewing and limit shows with violent themes?	Y	S	N
Do you often watch TV with your child?	Y	S	N
Do you discuss television programs with your child?	Y	S	N

MOVIES
Do you know what's on the screen at the theater?

	Go	Caution	Stop
Do you make sure you know what movies your child is going to see at the theater?	Y	S	N
Does your child need your permission before seeing a movie?	Y	S	N
Do you check movie ratings before giving permission?	Y	S	N

	Go	Caution	Stop
Do you consult other movie evaluations besides the industry ratings to find out more about the content?	Y	S	N
Do you allow your child to see movies that contain a lot of violence?	N	S	Y

RADIO/CD
Does your child have his/her own radio or stereo?

	Go	Caution	Stop
Do you listen to the music your child is playing?	Y	S	N
Do you listen to the stations your child is tuning into?	Y	S	N
Do you talk to your child about lyrics that you object to?	Y	S	N
Does your family have age-appropriate limits on the types music your child purchases?	Y	S	N

COMPUTER GAMES
Check your game collection.

	Go	Caution	Stop
Do you own or rent games that have violent content? (Violence on the cover is a good clue as to the content.)	N	S	Y

Do you play the games so that you become familiar with the content?	Y	S	N
Are the games you buy age appropriate for your child?	Y	S	N
Do you check a game's rating before renting or buying?	Y	S	N
Do you limit your child's game-playing time?	Y	S	N

INTERNET
Does your child have access to the Internet at home?

	Go	Caution	Stop
Do you monitor computer use?	Y	S	N
Do you use an Internet-blocking device that prevents children from visiting inappropriate websites?	Y	S	N
Do you find and list appropriate sites?	Y	S	N
Have you talked with your child about the best use of the Internet?	Y	S	N

VIDEO GAMES
Check your home collection.

	Go	Caution	Stop
Do you own or rent games that have violent content? (If the cover has a violent scene, the content is probably violent.)	N	S	Y
Do you play the games so that you become familiar with the content?	Y	S	N
Do you rent a game to preview it before purchasing?	Y	S	N
Are your games age appropriate for your child?	Y	S	N
Do you check a game's rating before you rent or buy it?	Y	S	N
Do you limit your child's game playing time?	Y	S	N

VIDEOS
Do you own a VCR?

	Go	Caution	Stop
Do you monitor which movies your child picks out at the video store?	Y	S	N

Do you check movie ratings before allowing your child to choose a video?	Y	S	N
Do you consult other movie evaluations besides the industry ratings to find oud more about the content?	Y	S	N
Do you check with other parents about which videos may be shown at parties or sleepovers?	Y	S	N
Do you allow your child to see videos that contain a lot of violence?	N	S	Y

Look at your answers for each category.

> Answers circled in the **Go** (green light) column mean that your family is practicing positive media habits.

> Answers circled in the **Caution** (yellow light) column mean you might want to take time to review your family's media habits in these areas.

> Answers circled in the **Stop** (red light) column means you might want to think about changing your family's media habits in these areas.

As parents, it's our job to help our children reap the benefits of new media and avoid their pitfalls and traps. I hope that the preceding activities have raised your awareness of the media that surround us and made you consider how you can become more involved in choosing what does and does not belong in your children's media diet. As you read on, you'll find tools and ideas to help you create a media-smart family.

Chapter 2 continues to focus on the types of media we are exposed to every day, outside and inside our homes, and what impact this might have on our children.

Chapters 3 and 4 take a look at television, still the number one media of choice for most kids. An important activity here is the TV log to find out who's watching what and for how long. Chapter 4 will look at media messages, and focus on what actions you can take to foster healthy media use.

Chapter 5 focuses on the news and how to tell the difference between news and entertainment.

Chapter 6 takes a look at advertising and how advertising can affect your child.

In chapter 7, activities focus on the Internet and how to help your children practice safe computing.

Chapter 8 outlines how to choose a video game and build a family plan around healthy video game use.

Chapter 9 activities focus on the world of teen music. How to listen and learn can open up new avenues of communication with your teen.

Chapter 10 focuses on reading. A child's success in school is strongly affected by the amount and use of media in their lives. These activities encourage reading along with healthy media use.

CHAPTER TWO

• • • • • • • • • • •

The Power of Media

One of the things my wife and I thought was important as our kids were growing up was eating dinner together as a family. I know a lot of parents feel the same way. It wasn't an edict of the household so much as it was just the way we did things. Everyone looked forward to this comfortable gathering at the end of a busy day. However, sometimes actually getting the gang to the table wasn't as easy as calling out, "Dinner's ready." Not when something else had their attention. Growling bellies meant nothing when the television was on. I remember having to spread myself in front of the set just to get them to look at me; then I could work on getting them to listen. As they craned their heads to see around my legs, they'd start to realize I was there. If their dream state lingered any longer than I could stand, I took the ultimate step. The off button.

Sounds familiar, I'm sure. Every parent has witnessed the TV trance: *A bomb could go off and they wouldn't know it. The house could burn down. They turn into zombies.* We've all seen and said those things. We've even felt it, that momentary feeling in the pit of the stomach when we realize how mesmerized our children are in front of a screen. The phenomenon is not limited to TV. We see the same thing happen when our kids play video games, computer games, and cruise the Internet. How can media be so powerful? What is the draw?

Part of the answer has to do with our biology. To begin with, television and other visual electronic media appeal to our dominant sense: vision. All living creatures rely on a dominant sense, not to the exclusion of other senses, but in greater measure. A bear, for example, can detect an odor we would never notice. A beluga whale can hear fifty miles away via a highly developed sense of hearing. The human brain has more neurons dedicated to seeing than to the other four senses combined. Part of our attraction to electronic visual media is that it's a natural match for our dominant sense. The fact that it also involves another one of our senses—hearing—makes it all the more engaging.

We've witnessed the power of this attraction as our kids sit riveted in front of a TV or computer screen. Whether or not we're alarmed by it, we're certainly aware of it. Here's a story that illustrates just how strong the connection is between visual media and our dominant sense. It comes from an anthropologist who was living in Papua New Guinea in 1989, the year they turned television on there for the first time ever. He told me that if he hadn't been there to see it, he wouldn't have believed the change it made in village life. Prior to TV, people in the village spent their evenings talking with each other, telling stories, and reviewing events of the day. This social interaction was their entertainment. As soon as TV entered the scene, it became the focal point. With the flick of a button a generations-old custom of entertainment and interactive teaching disintegrated.

The average time spent in front of electronic screens (TV, computer, video games) is nearly four-and-one-half hours each day among two to seventeen year olds. (*Annenberg Public Policy Center,* 1999.)

Electronic visual media works on yet another aspect of our cerebral make-up—kind of a double whammy, if you will. Besides being visually dominant, our brains are also wired to pay attention to things that move. Psychologists call this the *ori-*

entation response. If you're reading a book and a mouse runs across the room, it is likely that you will notice it out of the corner of your eye. This orientation to movement is an innate survival mechanism, a protective tool in a world of prey versus predator: Things that move could be a threat, so we're designed to pay attention to them. Even though we don't depend on this trait in modern life as much as we once did, it remains a fundamental element of our physiology. Because television and other forms of visual media involve a lot of movement, they get our attention. In fact, it's almost hard *not* to pay attention. Children will literally stop what they are doing if a TV is on—you've probably seen this for yourself. One mother even told me that her five-month-old preferred looking at television to looking at his mother's face. If the TV was on, the baby immediately turned away from his mother and strained to see the screen. This is what we mean when we say that TV has *magnetic appeal.*

So, part of what makes visual media so powerful for kids is that it plays into their basic wiring. The rest of its power has to do with another facet of their design: how they learn. Anyone who's spent time around kids knows that like most living creatures they learn by copying what they see and hear. This is how they learn language, learn to write their names, and learn to socialize.

An interesting study involving bluebirds illustrates this. Soon after hatching, young bluebirds were removed from their nest. They were fed, sheltered, and otherwise physically cared for. They survived and matured. However, none of the birds ever learned to sing the bluebird's characteristic song. They grew up making noise, because that ability is innate. But, without an adult bluebird to imitate, they weren't able to learn how to sing like other bluebirds.

Knowing how this paradigm for learning works, you can see why television is such a natural teacher. TV presents a window into other worlds filled with casts of characters to copy. Just watch kids to see how effective it can be.

Several of my colleagues and I did just that. We gathered a group of preschoolers—girls and boys—in a playroom with a television set. With the help of a one-way window and concealed cameras, we observed them as they watched a videotaped segment of *Barney.* On a remote feed in another room their parents observed them, too. The children watched Barney with rapt attention, and joined him in singalongs and dancing. Their activity was happy, friendly, and gentle—a mirror image of the show they were viewing.

Then, we ran the test again, but this time substituting a *Power Rangers* videotape for the children to watch. As the Power Rangers engaged in physical combat, the children were entranced, much as they were with Barney. Again, it wasn't long before they began copying what they were seeing, but, this time, they were jabbing, kicking, and jousting, just like the Power Rangers. The children's voices became loud, their actions confrontational—girls as well as boys. Some parents were shocked to see this side of their children. One mother commented, "I've never seen her behave anything like this before." The experiment left little doubt about the ability of television to influence young children who learn the only way they know how: by observing and imitating what they see and hear. Incidentally, we ran the study on three separate occasions and, each time, the results were identical.

Now, if you find yourself wondering what damaging things your child has watched when you weren't looking, don't be too hard on yourself. Parenthood isn't about doing things perfectly, it isn't about doing things right every minute of every day of your child's life. You've no doubt been told this before, but it sometimes helps to hear it again. Parenting is about doing the best job you can with what you know, the resources you have, and whatever life throws into the mix. So, add this insight to your memory bank, where you can refer to it as you make decisions about how to care for your child in the Media Age.

A few statistics will give you an idea of how this natural

teacher fits into family life today. Once it was introduced, television established itself in American homes very quickly. In 1950, less than 10 percent of America's families had TVs. By 1960, the percentage had risen to more than 90 percent. Today, more than 99 percent of American families have TVs— more than have telephones or flush toilets. The average American family has 2.6 sets. Fifty-six percent of our school-age children have a TV in their bedroom—translated, 56 percent have a private tutor. In the average family, the TV is on six hours a day, which is more than anyone is watching it. It is absolutely entrenched in our lives. And, for advertisers, that's a very good thing.

Advertisers know how powerful this natural teacher is. They count on it. If what we know about our own physiology and how kids learn isn't enough to support the idea that media are powerful, a look at corporate advertising budgets should tell us something. Money speaks loud and clear. The willingness of corporations to spend enormous sums to get their message into media indicates big confidence in its power to teach and influence. Super Bowl advertising is a prime example. To air one thirty-second spot during the 2000 Super Bowl cost a record $2.2 million. The network had no trouble selling all the spots. And the price escalates every year. As of this writing, the announced price of ads during the 2001 Super Bowl

> • • • • • • • • •
> The average American child grows up in a home with two TVs, three tape players, three radios, two VCRs, two CD players, one video-game player, and one computer. (*Kids and Media in the New Millennium*, Kaiser Family Foundation, 1999.)
> • • • • • • • • •

is $3.4 million. Of course, the spending trend isn't limited to special events; the same is true of advertising during regular TV programming and on the radio. Although the numbers aren't as big, they're just as revealing (chapter 6 provides the specifics on advertising spending in media).

So, where does this leave us? We could say at the mercy of

media's power and the advertisers who use it. As adults, however, we have the capacity to understand the facts and implications. We can make the decision to turn off the TV (or radio), mute the sound, change the channel, or not watch at all. Because our children can't, or don't, always act in their own best interest, we have to be their guides. We do this in all kinds of ways every day. We tell them to look before crossing the street, to wear a jacket because it's chilly, to save the treats for after a meal, and so on. Contending with the power of media is another part of defining how to care for them.

It makes sense, then, to think about the place media occupy in kids' lives today. There's a lot to think about. Media are everywhere. Just consider the places you can watch television outside your home: in restaurants, at the health club, in the airport, on a plane, in the car. Even while pumping gas—some new filling stations are now adding this benefit at the pumps. Your kids can watch while getting a haircut—a popular kids' salon in my neighborhood features a row of TV sets for young patrons getting a trim. The pervasiveness of media isn't limited to television. Now there are Internet cafes where you can surf the net while you eat. Internet laundromats let you surf while you wait for your clothes to dry. Personal-entertainment centers in airplane seats let you play games and watch videos while you cross the miles. You can watch movies on a chartered bus. As soon as there's a way to secure screens in bus stops, media will be there, too.

This proliferation of media is all the more powerful because it continues to evolve. New doesn't replace old; it just adds to the array of options. Television, for example, added to the communication and entertainment medium of radio. In the same way, studies show that video games and the Internet are not replacing TV; they are extending the possibilities. What this means for

• • • • • • • •

The television set in a child's bedroom is more often than not wired for cable or attached to a VCR or to a video-game player.

• • • • • • • •

our children is that the amount of time they spend using media is growing. As I mentioned earlier, kids today spend more time with media than doing anything else during their waking hours. All indications point to a media-saturated generation. Here's how the average school-age child spends time each week:

.5 hours interacting one on one with father
2.5 hrs. interacting with mother
5 hrs. doing homework
26 minutes reading outside school
25 hours watching TV

All the examples we've considered so far focus on visual media, which is not to suggest that other media aren't powerful or worth our concern. Visual media represent a larger portion of the pie, and, so, provide more ground to cover. Later, this book will devote an entire chapter to the impact of music on kids today (see chapter 9).

What we know about the power of media can be summed up this way: Media are natural teachers; media are everywhere; media occupy a majority of our kids' lives. Together, this is quite a potent mix. As parents, as caregivers, it is essential that we pay attention to this, that we recognize the implications. The underlying truth is this: Whoever tells the stories, defines the culture. Herein lies the ultimate power of media.

We all have ancestries rich in storytelling. From ancient campfire gatherings to more recent kitchen-table talks, stories have been used to recount news of the day with a bit of drama, humor, or exaggeration. Others were for entertainment or teaching a moral lesson. Some were forgotten in minutes, while others survived for thousands of years, passed on from generation to generation.

One of the enduring powers of storytelling is its ability to teach cultural norms and values. Stories provide a very effective tool for communicating what is and is not important to a group. Stories identify our heroes and the characteristics that give them that status. For example, *The Little Engine That Could* emphasizes the power of perseverance and a positive outlook. *The Three Little Pigs* underlines the importance of doing a job well and thoroughly.

While the role of storytelling in defining culture has remained constant for thousands of years, it has undergone a monumental change in recent decades. We have delegated more and more of the storytelling function to mass media, especially television. This has critically changed who tells the stories, how they are told, and what they tell. Parents, grandparents, teachers, pastors, authors, and sages have been replaced as the primary storytellers by teams of Hollywood scriptwriters, producers, and directors. Tales told in gatherings, or read under covers late at night, have been replaced by multimillion-dollar electronic productions. In turn, stories that were once told to teach important values have been replaced by whatever boosts ratings and sells products. Advertising runs the show (and shows). With such a significant shift in the purpose of storytelling, we have to wonder about how this storytelling is defining our culture. In the next chapter, we'll look closely at the phenomenon of advertising-driven TV, and the messages being taught to our children.

First, let's fill in more of the signposts and landmarks on our Cyberhood map. While the power of media to define cultural norms is impressive, parents can be very powerful, too. The activities that follow help us focus our attention on where the media are in our lives, how often we see media messages, and what the value messages are. We can fill in our map to healthy media use by being more aware of the values of messages of media and deciding whether those are the values we want our children to have.

• • • • • • • • • • • •

CHAPTER TWO ACTIVITIES

Activity: Media in the Media

For parents and teens.

We've been taking a look at the different types of media that surround us at home and in the community.

We also should be aware of the examples of media within the media (for example, a character in a movie watching television). Sometimes the media in the media provide companies with more opportunities to advertise their products. Being aware of this additional avenue of advertising highlights how lines between programming and advertising are breaking down.

For this activity, select two thirty-minute prime-time television shows or a video to watch with teen and adult members of your family. Work together as a team. You'll need a notepad and a pencil or pen.

1. Before you start, define what we mean by *media*.

    Media are the ways messages are carried from one person or group to another. This message can take many forms.

2. You will be viewing sixty minutes of prime-time television or part of a movie to find as many examples of media that are within the media that you are watching.

3. List each example. Examples include characters wearing T-shirts with messages or logos, listening to the car radio, banners, and so on.

• • • • • • • • • • • •

● ● ● ● ● ● ● ● ● ● ● ●

4. When the sixty minutes are up, review the list. How long is your list? What did you find? Did you notice media that you might not previously have seen?

Activity: Media by the Mile

For parents and children ages six through twelve.

In the last chapter you made a Media Map of the electronic media in your home. Now let's take a look at the different kinds of media we encounter when we step out the door.

Materials needed: Pen and paper (or this book).

If you live near a commercial section of your community, you may want to walk. If not, use your car and drive around the busier parts of your town or city for a half-hour.

Make a list of all the different types of media you can spot.

Remember, media are anything that is trying to communicate a message to you, so don't forget bus shelter signs, billboards, and so on. Also, what about that radio in the car?

_____   _____   _____

_____   _____   _____

_____   _____   _____

_____   _____   _____

_____   _____   _____

(Compare to answers on the next page.)

● ● ● ● ● ● ● ● ● ● ● ●

Did you find?

- Billboards
- Bus advertising
- Store signs
- Advertising signs on cars
- Flags/banners
- Bus shelters
- Video screens
- Shopping bag advertising
- Neon signs
- Electronic message boards
- Audio messages
- Flyers
- Posters

Activity: Media Types

For parents and children ages six and up.

Sometimes we think of media only in terms of TV and computers. This is another activity that will help you identify the multitude of ways in which messages are packaged and directed at us.

You will need blue and orange markers or crayons.

• • • • • • • • • • • •

Parent: Circle in blue the media that you see or hear almost every day.

Child: Circle in orange the media that you see or hear almost every day.

Remember: They may be in the background.

music tapes		magazines
brand logos	PARENT	billboards
videos		bumper stickers
CDs	CHILD	cereal boxes
radio		computer
television		newspapers
pagers		cell phones
video games		

Activity: Media Values

For parents.

Most parents say they want their child to grow up to be a "good" person. When asked to explain further they might say they want their child to be "honest," "hardworking," or "generous." As parents, we try to teach our children the values we think are important, but our children learn values from the broader culture also, and media play a big part in communicating those values. Sometimes, these media values are positive; other times, they are not. What are children learning?

Write down five values that your family holds. Put a check before those that you feel media supports and reinforces.

• • • • • • • • • • • •

• • • • • • • • • • •

Write down five values that media is most likely to teach.

Your Family Values

1. <u>Respect</u>
_____

2. _____
_____

3. _____
_____

4. _____
_____

5. _____
_____

Media Values

1. <u>Put-downs</u>
_____

2. _____
_____

3. _____
_____

4. _____
_____

5. _____
_____

Activity: Media Messages

For parents and children ages eight and older.

We've read now about media as natural teachers of our children. But what messages are they teaching? Whether positive or negative, these messages are powerful.

List three media (for example: television, radio, etc.) and write down two positive and two negative messages we or our children receive from each.

• • • • • • • • • • •

MEDIA	POSITIVE MESSAGES	NEGATIVE MESSAGES
1. _____	1. _____ _____ _____ 2. _____ _____ _____	1. _____ _____ _____ 2. _____ _____ _____
2. _____	1. _____ _____ _____ 2. _____ _____ _____	1. _____ _____ _____ 2. _____ _____ _____
3. _____	1. _____ _____ _____ 2. _____ _____ _____	1. _____ _____ _____ 2. _____ _____ _____

Activity: There's More to Life Than Media

For parents.

We've talked about the pervasiveness of media in our children's lives. But what do our children do that does not involve media?

Write down all the activities your child was involved in this past week that did *not* involve television, movies, videos, computers, video games, music, or radio.

Child 1	Child 2	Child 3
___	___	___
___	___	___
___	___	___
___	___	___
___	___	___
___	___	___
___	___	___
___	___	___
___	___	___
___	___	___

Tip: School is not media free. Don't count homework if the TV, CD player, or radio is on!

Activity: Screens, Screens Everywhere

For parents and children ages seven and older.

Television and video screens are popping up in more and more places. Each screen is directing advertising, information, or entertainment messages to us. Sometimes it's a combination of all three. One of the powers of media is that they are everywhere.

Think of all the places in the community you can find video screens trying to inform you or trying to sell you something.

_____   _____

_____   _____

_____   _____

_____   _____

_____   _____

_____   _____

_____   _____

_____   _____

_____   _____

Compare to answers on the next page.

Did you find screens in?

- Grocery stores
- Banks
- Dental offices
- Sports arenas
- Department stores
- Malls
- Restaurants
- Museums
- Car dealers
- Gas station pumps
- Hair salons/barbers
- Doctors' offices
- Airports
- Theme parks
- Art galleries
- Waiting rooms
- Cars

CHAPTER THREE

• • • • • • • • • •

Television

> *Television will be the test of the modern world.*
> *For in this new opportunity to see beyond*
> *the range of our vision we shall discover either*
> *a new and unbearable disturbance of the*
> *general peace, or a saving radiance in the sky.*
> *We shall stand or fall by television.*
>
> ——E. B. White, 1938

I have read these prophetic words countless times to audiences around the country, and every time I feel a sense of awe. More than the substance of White's prediction, or the haunting aura of his foresight, what I find most amazing is that he wrote these daring observations a full decade before television would be available to the mass market, and several decades before its inexhaustible potential would be realized.

The technology for television was invented in 1929. It was in the midthirties that author E. B. White saw it for the first time at an exhibition. This beloved creator of *Charlotte's Web*, so perceptive about children, immediately saw the capacity of television to shape an entire society. However, the power of this technology would remain a mystery for a few more years; as we know, the world had more pressing issues at hand.

Nineteen twenty-nine is, of course, the year the stock-market crash sent the entire world into a depression. While the world's nations were preoccupied with economic woes and a Second World War, the incredible invention of television sat idle. When the war finally ended, and the Great Depression along with it, Americans felt tremendous relief, but there was some understandable uneasiness. With an economy that had been dedicated to supporting a war, and millions returning in need of jobs, there was a legitimate fear of slipping back into a depression. Americans needed a new unifying focus. What they had was a wealth of technology leftover from the war effort, and it was just the thing to build on to push the country forward. It was time for television.

What a debut it had. Everything came together at once to fuel the explosion of television—economic prosperity, a need to remain united, and emerging technology. The amazing phenomenon of television wasn't a matter of timing and technology alone. When television burst onto the market in the postwar era, it came paired with a mighty partner: advertising.

The marriage of media and advertising wasn't new; it had been successfully tried twice before. The model was first put to the test in the early nineteenth century, with the medium of print. Newspapers and magazines of the time began selling page space to businesses as a way of subsidizing the costs of publication. It worked beautifully. When radio entered the scene in the early twentieth century, it seemed natural to apply the model to this medium as well: Media and advertising remained happily paired. So, with the advent of television technology, advertising had a new dance partner. However, this time around, expectations for success were, at first, tentative. Television was still so new to the world, and more important, to advertisers.

I remember talking about this with Bob Keeshan, best

known by generations of kids as Captain Kangaroo. Many don't recall that before his role as the Captain, his first foray into television was as Clarabell the clown on *The Howdy Doody Show*. Those first days of television were so speculative, Keeshan explained, that his initial contract as Clarabell was only a month-long commitment. The powers in charge were waiting to see if they could really draw audiences and advertisers to TV. Of course, they didn't have to wait long. Success was immediate. Television proved the most powerful sales vehicle yet.

In 1948, the three networks that dominated television for decades were formed: CBS, ABC, and NBC. Under their direction, the first television programming filtered into the market. By 1950, just over four years after the war ended, televisions were still a luxury; only one family in ten owned a set. This exciting new technology was a toy for the wealthy. However, all of this changed in just a decade, thanks to the potent combo of television and advertising. As advertisers fed enormous sums of money into the networks by buying ad space for their products, the networks, in turn, were able to produce some very impressive TV programs. The price of TV sets came down quickly, making them affordable for the average American family. By 1960, 90 percent of American households had a TV set. Television had quickly become a mainstream fixture.

Although, from its earliest days, television was marked as a sales tool, Americans were largely unconscious of this fact. People were too busy taking in the wonder of television to pay much attention to the business model behind it. Television opened up new worlds as nothing else had. It was a science-fiction fantasy coming true. Shows like *Wide, Wide World*, hosted by Dave Garraway, left audiences marveling. From a studio in New York City, Dave Garraway would say, "today we're going to visit the Grand Canyon," and, instantly, the program would take viewers there and to other places around the world. These were exciting times. The thrill and magic of television were intoxicating. Television was a family event. It was knowledge brought to life. It was the best in entertainment.

And this is how the true purpose of commercial television was overshadowed for one generation, and a precedent set for many to come. Like television's first viewers, viewers today commonly believe the primary purpose of television is to entertain and inform. However, these are secondary goals, by-products of programming. The primary goal of television is, and always has been, to deliver eyeballs to advertisers—to keep you watching long enough for advertisers to get their message in front of you. If this sounds a bit overboard, it is, in fact, very much the truth. (The exception is, of course, public television, which is not tied to the advertising model; chapter 4 takes a look at the merits of this valuable asset.) Commercial television is a business, first and foremost. Remember how it began: an irresistible match between television and advertising. It was a good thing then, and it's even better now. Sophisticated technology has put the dazzle of television on a new level. The power of television to sell is unbeatable. And its mantra remains solidly intact: deliver eyeballs to advertisers.

This isn't just about the ads on television; their agenda is obvious. Programming is part of the scheme to sell, too: It's meticulously calculated and strategized to deliver viewers to advertisers. Consider those annoying commercial breaks; just when things get really interesting a program cuts to a slew of ads. Perfect timing. You've been hooked. Now, you want to stick around to see what's going to happen. In the meantime, you can take in a few commercials. Of course, these too are designed to keep you watching until show time resumes and the cycle can repeat itself.

Before this begins sounding too cynical, let's take a look at the math. The business formula behind television is very straightforward. As you probably know, ratings determine what we see on television; the more people watching a program, the higher the ratings. The higher the ratings, the more money networks can charge advertisers to air their spots. And, of course, the more money networks can charge, the more they can make. You can see how a Super Bowl spot gets sold for millions of dollars. Highly rated events and shows deliver lots of eyeballs to advertisers. As you also probably also know, high ratings don't necessarily imply high-quality messages. The quality of the message isn't the point. If you thumb through a trade publication aimed at television executives you won't see much ink given to the quality of programming. The talk is of eyeballs, ratings, and market share. The business of television is about bottom lines. If viewers didn't get advertisers' messages, the whole business of television would collapse.

This should raise a few parental antennae, since your kids watch television, too. Even if they're watching programming designed for kids, the same motivation to deliver eyeballs to advertisers holds true. Television is a business through and through. Children are valued as consumers, not as learners. A handful of high-quality programming aside, whatever messages your child does pick up in the process of watching TV are of secondary importance. If the messages happen to be positive—as some are—that's fine. If the messages happen to be negative—as too many are—then that's too bad. What matters most is the sale. Money is a powerful motivator. Whatever sells is fair game and, when it comes to selling, there's no vehicle like television to get the job done. The business of television has developed a self-perpetuating momentum all its own.

Nearly 16 minutes of advertising is found in an average hour of prime-time television.

Now that you know *what* television is doing, let's look at *how* it's doing it. Since the very existence of television depends on delivering eyeballs to advertisers, you can bet the networks have mastered the science of doing this. They know that the best way to get and hold your attention is to cause an emotional jolt. Psychologists have studied this phenomenon in depth. At the most basic level, the ability to respond emotionally is an innate part of the human survival mechanism. We are set up to react. Our emotions allow us to respond in a variety of ways—to feel sorrow or joy, fear, anger, desire, belonging, and so on. Television uses this to its advantage, stimulating our emotions in order to grab and hold our attention. The more powerful the emotional jolt, the more likely we are to keep watching. There are many ways to stimulate emotions in the viewers, but the business model favors those that are reliable and inexpensive. Three themes that fit that bill are violence, sex, and humor. It's not surprising that TV (and other media) is packed with this trio. If the goal of television were education or information, there wouldn't be as much violence, sex, or humor, but the goal is to capture attention. These three work like a charm in the service of that goal.

The effect of a given emotional jolt does have its limit, however. Once you've been exposed long enough to a particular jolt, you become desensitized to it. Desensitization leads to disinterest, which spells doom for advertisers. Of course, program producers can't let *that* happen. Instead, to keep your eyeballs aimed at the screen, programming increases the frequency as well as the intensity of the jolts. I call this the *jolts-per-show,* or JPS, factor. The higher the JPS factor, the better the chances of keeping you hooked until the inevitable com-

Thirty percent of children channel surf to select a show they want to watch. (*Measuring the Child Audience* Annenberg Public Policy Center, 1997.)

mercial break when the ad itself can work on your emotions. By boosting the frequency and intensity of the jolts per show, television hooks you from one moment to the next to ensure that you don't lose interest or use that magic wand—the remote control—to switch channels. A sure way to increase the intensity of an emotional jolt is to combine jolt factors: violence is often paired with sex or humor; sometimes a jolt involves all three. Combinations of jolts are becoming increasingly common in television (as well as in video games, computer games, and movies). It's no wonder our society often has skewed notions about death, love, and what's entertaining.

As if television weren't wielding enough power with emotional jolts, it comes at us with another bag of tricks—technical tricks. Here's where the brilliance of television production shines. Television uses an array of technical tricks to reinforce the emotional jolts, including pacing, camera angle, music, edits, volume, lighting, special effects, graphics, and animation. While you may not always realize it, these elements are hard at work fulfilling the goal of television. Nothing in television is an accident. Everything is carefully calculated to keep you watching. Emotional jolts grab and keep your attention; technical tricks reinforce their effect. It's not surprising we're so easily hooked—and our kids are just as susceptible.

Once they're hooked, their minds are open to whatever messages television is communicating. Even though the goal of television isn't to teach, a great deal of learning does take place because of the way kids learn: by observing and imitating what they see and hear. The most powerful kinds of messages are those that convey attitudes and values. Attitudes and values influence behavior. They reflect what's important, how to belong, how to feel, what decisions to make. As we'll see in chapter 4, some programs do communicate positive attitudes and values. If they were in the majority, you wouldn't have to worry so much about what your child is learning in front of the set. Unfortunately, the value messages of the marketplace—the messages that deliver eyeballs—are increasingly at odds with the values you know are important for raising a healthy child, and for maintaining a healthy society.

• • • • • • • •

Seventeen percent of children watch more than five hours of television every day. (Kaiser Family Foundation, 1999.)

• • • • • • • •

Television Myths and Facts

Myth: Television provides a good language model for young children.

Fact: Only an adult caregiver, interacting daily with a child, can provide a language model from which very young children can learn.

Myth: The dialogue used on television provides stimulation for children of all ages.

Fact: The approximate language grade level of television dialog is fourth grade.

Myth: Television has no effect on children.

Fact: Every activity of a child has an effect on their growing brains. Television occupies more waking time of an average child's life in the United States than any other activity.

Myth: The primary purpose of television is to inform and entertain.

Fact: The primary purpose of television is to deliver an audience to advertisers.

Myth: Very young children do not pay any attention to what is on the TV screen.

Fact: Children as young as fourteen months will imitate what they see on TV.

Myth: More TVs in the house means less fighting over program choice.

Fact: More TVs in the house means more unregulated viewing by children.

Myth: Ultimately, children set their own viewing hours.

Fact: Parents determine whether a child will be a light viewer, moderate viewer, or a heavy viewer.

•   •   •   •   •   •   •   •   •   •   •

Myth: No television programs are good for preschool children.
Fact: Well-thought-out, educational programming made especially for preschool children can have a positive effect on school readiness skills and vocabulary acquisition.

Myth: Parents have no effect on how their child perceives television.
Fact: A child is greatly influenced by what their parents say about the reality of what they are watching on TV.

Myth: How different groups are portrayed on TV doesn't really have any effect in real life.
Fact: Children and teenagers report that television is one of their main sources of information about different ethnic groups.

•   •   •   •   •   •   •   •   •   •   •

For example, we say that violence is harmful, yet television and other media often promote it as exciting, glamorous, even funny, often the solution to a so-called hero's problem. Violence is so prominent in media today that the average American child will witness two hundred thousand acts of violence before graduating from high school.

Sex is another favorite media theme that makes statements to our kids. According to a *TV Guide* study, the average child in the United States will receive forty-five thousand messages about sex from television during their formative years. Media portrayals of sex are loaded with value statements most parents would find incompatible with their own, including: sex is only about fun, not commitment; sex is cool; just say "yes."

Frequent messages about wealth are hard to miss, like the key to happiness is money and what it can buy. We expect such materialism from commercials, but programming is just as guilty. Consider the economic status of most television characters; it far exceeds that of typical Americans. Many of these characters don't even seem to work for a living or, if they do, the amount of time they spend doing a job is unrealistic. Which sends another value message: Get the rewards without the work. Along the same lines, commercials put a premium on individual happiness. Translated: selfishness. We don't have to wonder why. Getting us—and our kids—to acquire things is what the medium of television is after. These kinds of messages underscore the idea that whoever tells the stories, defines the culture.

Once it has been dissected and scrutinized, it's hard to think about television the same way. It's hard *not* to think about the strategies and priorities, too often at odds with what you value as a parent, that are being aimed at your child. It's unsettling to realize that such power is available to your child with the click of a button. As a parent you have to look at television in this honest light. In doing this, you gain the understanding to decide how television will be used—and enjoyed—in your child's life.

Television will continue to use themes that get our attention and keep us watching. It will continue to send messages, for better or worse, as a by-product of its effort to sell. Our children will continue to learn whatever television has to teach unless we take it upon ourselves to *actively* care about what that is. This doesn't mean that television must amount to something that is good or bad; what is important is to recognize that television is powerful. It is our job to use what we know to make responsible decisions about television for our children. It should be our goal to help them learn for themselves how to use television appropriately. By being more discerning about viewing choices and habits we can weed through less worthy options, and take advantage of the gems that do come along.

Forty-four percent of children and teens report watching different programs when their parents are not around. (*Pediatrics,* January, 1999.)

The goal of the following activities (as well as those in chapter 4) is to help families make a plan for television viewing. The focus here is on the what, where, when, and how of TV use.

The first step in creating a plan is to log the viewing hours and shows of different members of the family. Next you will fill out Questions to Think About. Based on your TV log, you'll be able to decide if there are any areas of concern in the amount of viewing or when it occurs. The list of TV myths and facts gives some food for thought. The last two activities help us to understand why television is so powerful in attracting and holding our attention.

CHAPTER THREE ACTIVITIES

Activity: Television Log

For parents or parents with children ages seven and up.

Sometimes the television is just on in the background, or maybe we turn it on when we are bored. Some of us are news or sports fans, while others can't wait for that favorite drama. Before we can make a media plan for our family (at the end of chapter 4), it's a good idea to get a handle on what and how much television our family watches.

Use the log to record the television programs, who's watching, and for how long, for several days, up to a week. If you have more than one TV you may want to make a copy of this log and keep one by each set.

Note: If you are channel surfing and did not watch just one program, fill in "surfing" under TV Program.

MONDAY

Time of Day	Name of TV Program	Who's Watching Parent	Child	Where	Total Time
___	___	___	___	___	___
___	___	___	___	___	___
___	___	___	___	___	___
___	___	___	___	___	___
___	___	___	___	___	___
___	___	___	___	___	___

TUESDAY

Time of Day	Name of TV Program	Who's Watching Parent	Child	Where	Total Time
___	___	___	___	___	___
___	___	___	___	___	___
___	___	___	___	___	___
___	___	___	___	___	___
___	___	___	___	___	___
___	___	___	___	___	___

WEDNESDAY

Time of Day	Name of TV Program	Who's Watching		Where	Total Time
		Parent	Child		
――――	――――――	――――――	――――――	――――	――――――
――――	――――――	――――――	――――――	――――	――――――
――――	――――――	――――――	――――――	――――	――――――
――――	――――――	――――――	――――――	――――	――――――
――――	――――――	――――――	――――――	――――	――――――
――――	――――――	――――――	――――――	――――	――――――

THURSDAY

Time of Day	Name of TV Program	Who's Watching		Where	Total Time
		Parent	Child		
――――	――――――	――――――	――――――	――――	――――――
――――	――――――	――――――	――――――	――――	――――――
――――	――――――	――――――	――――――	――――	――――――
――――	――――――	――――――	――――――	――――	――――――
――――	――――――	――――――	――――――	――――	――――――
――――	――――――	――――――	――――――	――――	――――――

FRIDAY					
Time of Day	Name of TV Program	Who's Watching Parent	Child	Where	Total Time
_____	_____	_____	_____	_____	_____
_____	_____	_____	_____	_____	_____
_____	_____	_____	_____	_____	_____
_____	_____	_____	_____	_____	_____
_____	_____	_____	_____	_____	_____
_____	_____	_____	_____	_____	_____

SATURDAY					
Time of Day	Name of TV Program	Who's Watching Parent	Child	Where	Total Time
_____	_____	_____	_____	_____	_____
_____	_____	_____	_____	_____	_____
_____	_____	_____	_____	_____	_____
_____	_____	_____	_____	_____	_____
_____	_____	_____	_____	_____	_____
_____	_____	_____	_____	_____	_____

SUNDAY					
Time of Day	Name of TV Program	Who's Watching Parent	Child	Where	Total Time
___	___	___	___	___	___
___	___	___	___	___	___
___	___	___	___	___	___
___	___	___	___	___	___
___	___	___	___	___	___
___	___	___	___	___	___

Activity: Questions to Think About

For parents.

With your completed TV log in hand, answer the following questions. Decide if there are any areas of concern regarding the amount of television viewing, where it occurs, or when it occurs.

On average, how many hours is the TV on each day?

_____

How many total hours is it on during the week?

_____

What time of day does your family watch the most television? _____

What time of day do your children watch the most television? _____

How many hours a day do your children watch television? _____

Who's watching the most television? _____

Where in the house are your children watching television? _____

List any areas of concern about your children's television viewing:

_____

_____

_____

Activity: Television Programming and You

For parents and children ages eight and up.

We've explained that the purpose of television is to deliver an audience to advertisers. One way to visualize this clearly is to watch different television programs and track what kinds of commercials are shown and who the intended audiences are.

Pick out three half-hour television programs. (Try to pick three shows that air at different times of day.)
- Using the chart below, list each program.
- List the commercials that run during the program you are watching.
- Identify the intended audience for each commercial.
- Watch the program and identify who you think the intended audience is for each program.

For example:

NAME OF PROGRAM	INTENDED AUDIENCE	COMMERCIALS	INTENDED AUDIENCE
Pokemon	children	toys cereal	children children

NAME OF PROGRAM	INTENDED AUDIENCE	COMMERCIALS	INTENDED AUDIENCE
1. _____	_____	_____	_____
	_____	_____	_____
	_____	_____	_____
	_____	_____	_____
	_____	_____	_____
2. _____	_____	_____	_____
	_____	_____	_____
	_____	_____	_____
	_____	_____	_____
	_____	_____	_____
3. _____	_____	_____	_____
	_____	_____	_____
	_____	_____	_____
	_____	_____	_____
	_____	_____	_____

Discussion: Why do you think commercials for children's toys aren't aired during evening dramas or football games?

Activity: Jolts and Tricks

For parents and children ages four and up.

Jolts and Tricks is designed to help you identify the emotional jolts and the technical tricks that television producers and advertisers use to get and keep our attention.

Videotape, if possible, several commercials or television shows so you can stop action or view sections again. Choose some commercials that are very popular. Below you'll record some of the jolts and tricks you and your children will spot together.

Suggestions for ages four to eight:
- Children in this age group may not understand the term *jolts and tricks,* or be able to differentiate between them. You can explain them as anything that makes them sit up and pay more attention. Stick to simple examples for jolts such as hitting, kicking, shooting people (violence); making people laugh (humor); and making people scared (fear). Simple examples of tricks include music and volume.
- Select two television programs that your child usually watches.
- Ask your child to look for just one or two jolts or tricks that he or she clearly understands. For example, have your child watch and/or listen for things that make people laugh.

• Watch the shows together and fill out the charts with your child.

Discuss:
• Why do they use jolts and tricks in television?
• What jolts and tricks does your child like? Dislike? Why?

Suggestions for ages nine to twelve:
• Children in this age category should be able to understand the difference between jolts and tricks and look for examples of both. Before your child watches the selected programs and fills out the Jolts and Tricks charts, watch a segment of a television program or commercial and work together to point out various jolts and tricks.
• Have your child invite a friend over to hunt for jolts and tricks with you.

Discuss:
• What is the goal of television?
• Why do the people who make television programs and commercials use jolts and tricks?

Suggestions for ages thirteen to eighteen:
• This age category should be able to understand the difference between jolts and tricks, as well as all the information presented in this chapter.
• Select and compare two programs and their commercials that were designed for different audiences.

Discuss:
- What is the intended audience of each show?
- How were the jolts and tricks in the two programs and their commercials similar or different? Why might this be?
- Does the use of jolts and tricks seem manipulative? Why or why not?

Jolts

First we'll look at the jolts. (Remember: *Jolts* are emotional hot buttons that grab and hold our attention.)

Circle the jolts used in the commercial or television program you are watching. (*Tip:* You may be circling a type of jolt more than once.)

Jolts/ Emotional Hot Buttons

Commercial	violence	fun	sex	hunger
_____	fear	excitement		danger
	joy	humor		sadness
Commercial	violence	fun	sex	hunger
_____	fear	excitement		danger
	joy	humor		sadness

Jolts/ Emotional Hot Buttons

Television Program	violence	fun	sex	hunger
_____	fear	excitement		danger
	joy	humor		sadness

Television Program	violence	fun	sex	hunger
_____	fear	excitement		danger
	joy	humor		sadness

Often, different jolts may be combined to create an even more intense emotional effect on the viewer.

Tricks

Now, we'll look at the technical tricks. Remember, these are the techniques that grab and hold our attention.

Circle the technical tricks used in the commercial or television program you are watching. You may be circling a technical trick more than once.

Technical Tricks

Commercial	special effects		pacing
_____	music	edits	color
	camera angles		volume
	lighting	makeup	graphics
Commercial	special effects		pacing
_____	music	edits	color
	camera angles		volume
	lighting	makeup	graphics

Technical Tricks

Television Program	special effects		pacing
_____	music	edits	color
	camera angles		volume
	lighting	makeup	graphics
Television Program	special effects		pacing
_____	music	edits	color
	camera angles		volume
	lighting	makeup	graphics

Different jolts and multiple tricks are often combined to create an even more intense emotional effect on the viewer.

Next, chapter 4 will add another layer to your TV smarts by looking more in depth at the effects of television on kids today—both positive and negative. You'll also explore several other timely issues: the state of children's television, kids and the news, ratings, and the V-chip.

CHAPTER FOUR

• • • • • • • • • • •

From *Sesame Street* to *South Park:*
What Kids Learn from Television

"She learned her ABCs from Big Bird," a beaming mother of a two-year-old repeated to me. "My son says he likes the color of his skin, because Elmo likes his red fur," a pleased father explained. Most parents of little ones recognize these lessons and lovable Muppets from the children's television program, *Sesame Street.* This ingenious creation began airing in 1969 and became a testament to the positive educational power of children's television. But it was a first.

In the 1950s, promises were made about the educational benefits of television. However, most children's programming was geared to entertain, rather than teach. The only real attempts to use television for teaching were aimed at high-school and college students. The industry constantly struggled between seemingly opposing desires: to explore the educational potential of television, and fulfill its commercial goals. Because television was immediately paired with advertising, as chapter 3 explains, the advertisers' agendas often overshadowed interest in the educational potential of the medium. Eventually, this tension led to the birth of public television. In 1967, the Public Broadcasting Act established a network of noncommercial stations dedicated to an educational agenda. You may remember that in the beginning public television was actually referred to as *educational television*.

The early offerings of educational television weren't very promising. Considered dull and disappointing, viewership was low. With the introduction of *Sesame Street,* the face of educational TV was remade. This landmark children's program marked the first time that educators, psychologists, and television professionals had come together to apply their talents to the goal of teaching children reading, cognitive skills, self-esteem, and positive social behavior. And it worked.

• • • • • • • •
Seventy-seven percent of all preschool children watch *Sesame Street* at least once a week. (U.S. Dept. of Education.)
• • • • • • • •

Hundreds of studies have demonstrated the educational benefits of *Sesame Street.* Its success led the way for the production of other high-quality children's educational programs. Shows like *The Electric Company* and *Reading Rainbow* were able to reach children across all socioeconomic groups, including children considered educationally disadvantaged. Some recent innovations in children's programming have continued to offer high-quality educational value, including *Blue's Clues, The Adventures of Little Bear,* and *Between the Lions.*

Since we know that television is a powerful teacher, we should expect that it could teach positive lessons, as these shows have done, and produce beneficial results. Of course, our expectation is tempered by what we know about television's motivation for profit, and by what the majority of programming has to offer—that is, very little. By considering ways in which television *can* have a positive effect on our children, we can choose programming which reflects these benefits accordingly. Television can help children:

Develop Cognitive Skills. Research shows that television can help children improve skills in reading, vocab-

Children's Books about TV

Storybooks can often start a conversation about a family's use of television. The following is a list of storybooks that will appeal to preschoolers and primary age children focusing on television and the family.

1. *The Berenstain Bears and Too Much TV*
   by Stan Berenstain, illustrated by Jan Berenstain, 1984.

   Mama Bear, feeling that the young bears are watching too much TV, bans the TV for a week. After initial protest, the bears create a lot of fun for themselves and the whole family.

2. *Better Than TV*
   by Sara Swan Miller, illustrated by Michael Chesworth, 1998.

   The TV shuts down after a power outage. Now the kids must rely on themselves and each other for play.

3. *Bionic Bunny Show*
   by Marc Tolon Brown, illustrated by Lauren K. Krasny, reprint 1985.

   A lesson on special effects *versus* reality, kids see how an ordinary bunny is turned into a bionic bunny for a TV show.

4. *Box-Head Boy*
   by Christine M. Winn and David Walsh, 1996.

   A boy becomes so involved with television that the TV becomes his head!

5. *Grandpa's Visit*
   by Richard Keens-Douglas, illustrated by Frances Clancy,
   1996.

A surprise visit by grandpa and a lesson for a young boy on the important things in life are the focus of this story.

6. *Mouse TV*
   by Matt Novak, 1994.

The mouse family loves to watch TV, but they also argue loud and long about what to watch. What happens when the TV breaks down?

7. *Aunt Chip and the Great Triple Creek Dam Affair*
   by Patricia Polacco, 1996.

Everybody forgets how to read when television comes to town. They even forget what books are for. Aunt Chip comes to the rescue.

8. *Take a Look, It's in a Book: How Television Is Made at Reading Rainbow*
   by Ronnie Krauss, illustrated by Christopher Hornsby,
   1997.

Take an inside look at the making of the television show, *Reading Rainbow*.

9. *Tom the TV Cat*
   by Joan Heilbroner, illustrated by Sal Murdocca, 1984.

Watching his owner's TV, Tom the cat tries to be different characters he sees on the screen.

10. *When the TV Broke* (Puffin Easy-To-Read, Level 1)
    by Harriet Ziefert, illustrated by Marvis Smith, 1993 reissue)

Jeffrey is faced with the problem of what to do when the TV breaks.

ulary, math, and problem solving. Even toddlers can learn to count and identify letters and colors.

Gain Academic Knowledge. Young children can learn from television programs about history, art, music, science, drama, literature, and many other subjects. Entire cable networks like The History Channel and The Discovery Channel have evolved as wonderful resources.

Learn Positive Behavior. Programs like *Barney & Friends* and *Touched By An Angel* demonstrate cooperation, caring, and good communication.

Understand Nutrition and Health. Television can be a major source of information about health-related topics. Public-service announcements and some advertisements may also be effective in promoting healthy eating habits and lifestyles.

Build Awareness of Current Events. People today are better informed about events and issues that shape society and the world than at any other time in history. This information is delivered through both news and entertainment programs. Dramatic presentations of issues such as family violence and poverty can raise awareness of problems and even spark movements to address them.

As you flip through the channels or peruse a *TV Guide* looking for programming with these kinds of benefits, the options are scarce. Islands of excellence do exist, but they float in a sea of disappointing fare. This imbalance is improving, if only slightly. In 1996, the Telecommunications Act was passed in an effort to increase the amount of educational programming available. According to the law, all broadcast networks are now required to provide three hours of educational programming per week, or lose their license to broadcast. In order to meet this requirement, programs must be specifically produced to educate children, to provide them with positive cognitive and social lessons. This means you should be able to find more educational programming for your child than ever before. These programs are identified in your *TV Guide* by the symbol E/I, for Educational/Informational. If you weren't aware of this symbol, you're not alone. In surveys done at the National Institute on Media and the Family only 4 percent of the parents in the United States recognized its meaning. Of course, the E/I designation does not imply that a program is high quality or that it is effective; it only means that it is intended as a positive educational vehicle for children as required by the act. You still have to judge the merits of a show for yourself, but the symbol does help focus your search.

> One in five E/I designated children's programs was found to have little or no educational value. (*The State of Children's Television,* Annenberg Public Policy Center, 1999.)

Violence

While television's potential to do good is far from realized in current programming, its adverse effects are abundant. Because television producers have made it their business to keep us watching by arousing our emotions, they surely know how to do it. One of the most effective devices in their toolbox is *violence*. The National Television Violence Study profiled programs across a broad range of channels and found that 57 percent of *all* shows and 66 percent of children's shows contained violence. Clearly, the networks are creating a lot of opportunities to get our attention. However, getting our attention isn't the only effect of violent entertainment. Hundreds of studies have cited violent entertainment as a cause of violent attitudes and behavior. Numerous professional organizations have gone on record saying that the evidence is overwhelming on this point (including the American Academy of Child and Adolescent Psychiatry, the American Academy of Pediatrics, the American Medical Association, the American Psychological Association, and The National Institutes of Health.) Media scholar Aletha Houston testified before Congress that "virtually all independent scholars agree . . . there is evidence that TV can cause aggressive behavior."

• • • • • • • • •

Children's programs are more likely to contain violence than general audience programs. (1998 State of Children's Television Report, Annenberg Public Policy Center, 1998.)

• • • • • • • • •

Study results and professional opinions certainly bolster the case against violent entertainment. However, most of us don't need these revelations to tell us what we already feel in our hearts every time we read a violent headline, watch our kids shove or hit each other like pro wrestlers, or hear them use the heartless motto of a Hollywood hero. Media violence is so prevalent that we *have* to consider how it affects the behavior and attitudes of our children. We have to take a hard look at the risks and realities of violent entertainment, especially television, because it is so accessible to our children on a daily basis.

At the most basic level, television violence models violent behavior. While kids imitate the positive social behavior they see in media, they also imitate the violent, aggressive behavior. Children as young as fourteen months begin imitating what they see on television. Children of all ages are drawn to models they like on television; the more appealing they find a particular character the more they will try to emulate the character's behavior. This is why violent heroes are even more harmful to children than violent villains. We even have a cliché to describe how violent acts become heroic in the hands of the good guy (and sometimes the bad guy): *glorified violence*. When violence is glamorized or depicted as a successful solution, it sends the message that violent acts are rewarded. And this increases the likelihood that violent behavior will be repeated in real life. *Justified violence* is another dangerous two-word phrase. Violence is all the more likely to be imitated if it also carries the message, "It's okay to resort to violence as long as you think you are justified." What child doesn't think he or she is right in a conflict?

Desensitization

Another fallout of television's steady stream of attention-grabbing violence is desensitization. You'll remember that we touched on this in chapter 3 when we looked at how emotional jolts are used to get our attention and keep us watching. As with any emotional jolt, constant exposure to television violence blunts our emotional reaction to it. Programming keeps it coming in more and more concentrated doses; each successive act of violence is more powerful than the last. And, 58 percent of the time, the victim isn't shown experiencing any pain (Mediascope, *National Television Violence Study,* 1998). Our kids get used to the escalating, consequence-free violence television dishes out. Violence becomes less jarring, less alarming, less *real.* Even in the *real* world. When their senses become numbed by a continual barrage of TV violence, the real thing isn't as shocking anymore. They just stop taking it seriously. Studies have shown that repeated exposure to media violence not only decreases our reaction to violence, but also our responsiveness to victims of attacks.

When we look at how realistic television violence is now, it's all the more alarming to realize how desensitized our kids are becoming: that someone being graphically blown to pieces or viciously attacked is all part of a routine day in TV land. It leaves you wondering how much more violent violence can get. Unfortunately, we have only to watch the screen (TV, computer, or movie) to find out. Our appetite for violence grows in direct proportion to our level of desensitization—

studies demonstrate this as well. So, scriptwriters and directors will gladly find a way to feed our hunger—keep in mind, this means our children's too—in order to keep us watching.

The World Is a Frightening Place

For parents of toddlers and preschoolers, television violence poses another risk. Because children this young are unable to differentiate between reality and fantasy, violence on TV makes the world look like a frightening place. Even cartoons or other animated stories often portray aggressive situations—however mild they may seem to us—that can be frightening to an impressionable young viewer. If you're like most parents, you've probably experienced this with your child at one time or another: an image on TV that was just too real, the ensuing emotional upset, nightmare, or repeated need for reassurance. Many of the Disney videos made for kids are too much for younger children; the good messages can be wonderful, but the inevitable conflicts which arise to keep the story going can be startling and scary.

We could go on and on about television violence and its effects; libraries and bookstores can offer plenty of additional material if you're interested in delving deeper. The point is to give you enough information that you can look at TV violence more critically and feel better equipped to make decisions about what your children watch.

This brief discussion does underscore the power of television violence to affect behavior. We know this is serious business. We can't help but worry about the negative impact media violence is having on the health and well-being of our kids. If they cease to be moved by the horror and gravity of violence, what does this mean for their ability to feel compassion, empathy, and remorse? If they are motivated to seek physical resolutions to conflict and desire, what does this mean for their safety and the safety of others? The stakes may even be higher than we think they are. The most harmful effect of this steady diet of violent entertainment may not be violent behavior. To me, the real tragedy is that it has created and nourished a culture of disrespect. For every kid in the news who picks up a gun, there are thousands who don't, but they're calling each other names, pushing, shoving, and hitting with increasing frequency. Television and its media counterparts have redefined how we're supposed to treat one another. We've gone from "have a good day" to "make my day." Our kids have not missed this lesson.

> The average American child sees 16,000 murders on television by the age of eighteen. *(American Medical Association)*

The V-Chip: A Solution?

Understandably, concern about violence on television has been growing for years. With the Telecommunications Act of 1996 and its promise of V-chip technology, many parents are hoping a solution is just around the corner. The V-chip will allow parents to block out programs which are inappropriate for children. The V stands for violence, but the chip will also let parents block out programs with undesirable sexual content, vulgar language, and other unacceptable material.

Unfortunately, the V-chip isn't likely to come to our rescue the way we'd like—either quickly *or* completely. V-chip technology is a standard feature in TV sets produced after January 1, 2000. Since the average life of a TV is seven to ten years, it will be quite awhile before most families make the expenditure for a set with V-chip technology. Retrofitting a TV to handle V-chip technology is cost-prohibitive and requires cumbersome external equipment.

Hardware issues aside, there is also concern about the effectiveness of the V-chip. Technically, the V-chip works based on a system of ratings. Parents are supposed to use the ratings to decide which programs they wish to block out, then enter corresponding code numbers via a TV remote. The V-chip will read the codes and block the designated shows. However, the V-chip will only be as good as the ratings system, which already is getting its share of criticism from parents and others concerned about the media health of America's children. The ratings system currently in place was devised by the television industry and based on the ratings used by the motion picture industry. And, like movie ratings, the word from many parents is that TV ratings aren't strict enough. This seems to be especially true of the TV 14 rating assigned to programs deemed suitable for children age fourteen and up. The majority of parents surveyed on the issue feel that TV 14 shows should instead receive the M rating which identifies *mature* programs appropriate for age seventeen or older.

In answer to the inadequacies of the industry ratings system, the National Institute on Media and the Family developed an alternative media ratings system called *KidScore*. Its content-based evaluations of TV programs and video games are based on national research with parents and child-development experts—none of whom have any connection to the entertainment industry. As a result, KidScore addresses the issues most parents said they cared about. It evaluates television programs, videos, and video games on two levels: appropriateness for different age categories; and amount of violence, vulgar language, sexual content, and illegal or harmful behavior. In a matter of seconds, parents can get the full picture. You can check out KidScore ratings at www.mediafamily.org. It is our hope at the institute that KidScore and other alternative ratings systems will be widely available to parents in the near future.

If the industry ratings system remains the chosen partner for the V-chip, time will tell whether or not parents agree with its evaluations and use it effectively. Time will also tell if the invention will backfire by giving the networks license to push the limits of objectionable material further. Even in the best possible outcome, the V-chip is still a tool for parents—not a solution. As you probably realize, nothing can take the place of your involvement in your child's media experiences.

Messages About Sex

While television violence attracts a lot of attention from parents, educators, and health professionals, for many, the concern at the top of the list is sexual content and behavior in TV programming. A survey conducted by The National Institute on Media and the Family in 1996 found that parents were slightly more concerned about sex on TV than violence. This isn't surprising in light of the prevalence of sexual material on television; more sexual dialogue and behavior is depicted than violence. This trend has gained tremendous momentum in the last two decades. The number of primetime programs with sexual content or behavior increased by 74 percent from 1976 to 1996. By 1996, 75 percent of prime-time programs contained either sexual dialogue or sexual behavior. Clearly, there's ample reason for parents to be concerned.

However, it isn't just the frequent depictions of sex on television which many parents find disturbing. It's *how* sex is depicted. How television deals with sex sends powerful messages to the most impressionable among us: our children. A *TV Guide* study of daytime television programming is case in point: In 94 percent of the programs in which sexual behavior was depicted or alluded to, *none* of the characters involved were married. For children, trying to figure out how the world works, and therefore, *how they should behave*, the message here does more than devalue the institution of marriage. It communicates a host of sexual and moral values: sex is no big deal, do it whenever and with whomever, responsibility and consequences are unimportant. Realities like sexually transmitted diseases, unintended pregnancies, and moral implications are seldom dealt with on television. When they are addressed, their importance is often fleeting, overshadowed by the preponderance of more glamorous depictions of sex as fun, carefree, powerful, even prestigious.

Casual sex is routinely depicted in prime-time sitcoms like *Friends* and *Frasier,* and in *Seinfeld* reruns. While these and other programs might be entertaining for adults, as parents, we have to reconsider how their sexual messages affect our kids. This may seem obvious but, in practice, it isn't always so easy to do. Humor has an insulating effect. Because the combination of sex and humor makes light of sexual issues and situations, we're easily lulled into feeling that what we're watching is safe when the kids are around, that it isn't that bad, or that the kids probably won't get it anyway. But, for developing minds, often it is that bad, and they do get more of it than we'd like to think.

Moreover, the pairing of sex and humor is so common on TV that we're just plain used to it; we've become desensitized to the messages. Even television characters are often nonplussed by the implications of their own actions. One particular episode of *Frasier* comes to mind. The likable lead, Frasier, strikes up conversation with a woman at a department store. The attraction is evident and they make plans to go out on a date that evening. The next thing we know, they are at a restaurant, menus in hand, when the woman unabashedly asks Frasier if he wants to have sex. So much for dinner. The show concludes with Frasier coming from his bedroom, clad in almost nothing, the sexual encounter with the woman he met hours before clearly implied. Just at that moment Frasier's father, brother, and housekeeper arrive home. As a viewer, you expect the moment to be awkward (at least). However, no one is at all embarrassed, not even Frasier. Everyone treats the situation as status quo. The message is that casual sex is acceptable. All the fun without the responsibility. It's one of the most pervasive messages about sex in programming today.

Even when TV sex lives do involve consequences, they rarely reflect reality. You may recall the *Murphy Brown* episode

which garnered so much press a few years ago. Finding herself
single and pregnant, the character Murphy Brown eloquently
defended single mothers and the choice of unmarried women
to have children. But that depiction of a single mother—a
high-paying executive job, lavish home, and few responsibili-
ties other than fulfilling personal desires—is anything but accurate. The actual number of single mothers in the United
States with incomes greater than fifty thousand dollars a year
(and Murphy's was certainly *a lot* higher), is less than one
tenth of one percent of unwed mothers. Adults may realize
the discrepancy between fiction and fact; but how many kids
can see past the model life of a TV character to recognize that
the value being conveyed—in this case, sex without consequences—isn't based in reality?

Stereotypes

In the same way that TV portrayals of sex communicate
values parents find hard to swallow, television has a powerful
hand in creating stereotypes we might not want to promote either. TV commonly exposes us to stereotypes of ethnic and
racial groups, occupations, gender, and sexual orientation
which are, at the very least, inaccurate, and frequently, offensive. Without firsthand knowledge of a certain group of people, we can be susceptible to forming opinions based on how
that group is portrayed on television. TV may even be the only
source of information. Children, therefore, with their limited
frame of reference, are especially vulnerable to the influence
of stereotypes.

Even when we do have direct experience, television has the
power to shape our attitudes and behavior. Gender stereotypes are a good example. Despite the fact that all of us have
experience dealing with both sexes, television has the power to
create gender stereotypes which we subconsciously incorporate into our own gender belief systems. And, once we believe
in a stereotype, we are more likely to adjust our behavior to fit

our perceptions. Early adolescents are particularly easy targets for gender stereotyping on television. As they undergo tremendous physical change and are filled with confusing emotions, young girls and boys look to others to tell them how to look and behave. Naturally, the ever-accessible TV offers an abundance of perfect role models and heroes for comparison. Without realizing it, kids incorporate messages about what it means to look and behave like a man or a woman, what it means to be attractive. They watch and compare, and, inevitably, come up short. Things that are a normal part of development, like blemishes, awkward growth spurts, and weight gain, are measured against TV ideals: actors and actresses chosen not because they are normal but because they are unusually attractive. Popular teen shows like *Beverly Hills 90210* and *Melrose Place* are prime examples. These programs parade beautiful young people about as if they are the norm.

Messages About Gender

For young girls, one of the most potentially damaging gender messages alive in media today is that thin is beautiful. For boys, the message is that the more muscle, the better. Kids take messages like this to heart because beauty is promoted throughout media as the ground rule for worth, power, and success. Given those messages, the epidemic of eating disorders and steroid use in this country is not all that surprising.

Virtually all the experts on eating disorders point to media's powerful image of the ideal woman as one of the contributing factors. The typical woman on TV keeps getting lighter and lighter; so, the weight gap between the ideal woman and an actual woman keeps widening. A 1996 study found that the amount of time an adolescent watches soaps, movies, and music videos is associated with their degree of body dissatisfaction and desire to be thin (*International Journal of Eating Disorders*, 1996).

Other Health Risks

Messages about body ideals aren't the only health risks associated with television. Watching TV is, by nature, a sedentary activity (couch potatoes don't run marathons). When kids sit glued to the tube, they're giving up time that could be spent in more physical pursuits. While they sit, they're also captive for the onslaught of ads promoting unhealthy eating habits: snacking on high-fat, high-salt foods, or simply overeating. With the average American child spending more waking hours watching TV than doing anything else, it's no wonder that increased viewing is proving to be a risk factor for childhood and adolescent obesity.

Watching television is also a solitary activity, and thus has implications for social development. You don't need to have meaningful contact with other people in order to watch TV. While everyone can relate to the relief of zoning out for a bit, the concern for kids is that racking up hours in front of the set

> The more time children spend watching TV, the fatter they tend to be. (*Journal of the American Medical Association,* April, 1998.)

on a daily basis takes away from the development of social and interpersonal skills that come with human interaction. These are tools your children will depend on throughout life. Not only are kids missing out on real-life interactions when they watch TV, but they are soaking up the lessons in communication TV characters have to teach. If we don't agree with so many of the value messages being promoted on television, we shouldn't expect the interactions of TV characters to be shining examples either.

We've spent most of this chapter looking in broad strokes at the negative lessons TV is teaching our children. Any of the issues—violence, sex, stereotypes, gender messages, or health risks—are a book or more in themselves. And of course, there are other negative lessons to be had. What we have covered, however, should jump-start your TV awareness quotient, so that you can begin thinking about programming options more critically. This means looking for the good in television as well. Although the potential of TV to teach positive lessons got less ink, in light of so many concerns about the adverse effects, we shouldn't forget that there are programs worth watching and learning from.

The following activities can help you get started on sorting the good from the bad. The goal of these is to construct a TV plan that promotes good TV use in your family.

First, we'll take a look at the positive and negative messages your children receive from their favorite television shows. Next, you'll really dig into the content of programs by completing a KidScore rating. This will then prepare you to create a Family Television plan. Other stops along the road to healthy media use include creating an Alternative to TV activities list and educating yourself about the V-chip and industry TV Parental Guidelines.

CHAPTER FOUR ACTIVITIES

Activity: Television Messages

For parents.

In the previous chapters, we looked at the positive and negative messages we hear from media as a whole. In this chapter, as we focus on television, we need to ask ourselves what are the messages we are receiving from individual programs that we watch.

Choose a television program that your child watches. (If you have more than one child, choose a program that the older children watch and one that the younger children watch.)

Write up to three positive and up to three negative messages that your child may be receiving from that show.

NAME OF PROGRAM _____

Positive Messages   Negative Messages

1. _____   1. _____

   _____   _____

2. _____   2. _____

   _____   _____

3. _____   3. _____

   _____   _____

Activity: KidScore Rating

For parents.

The National Institute on Media and the Family has offered an alternative KidScore™ [1] rating for many media products, including television shows. Rated by parents like yourselves, KidScore offers parents another resource to help make good media choices for their children. (KidScore ratings are found at the National Institute on Media and the Family's website: http://www.mediafamily.org)

It has been noted that one of the negative effects of the barrage of media violence is that our children will become desensitized, and that in-your-face behavior will spill over into their own lives.

In this activity, we'll take a closer look at a television program and rate it using the categories from KidScore.

Pick out a television program that your child regularly watches that you might have some concern about. Try a Saturday morning cartoon show or a prime-time program that kids watch such as any one of the professional wrestling programs (*Smackdown, Raw Is War,* etc.).

In each category, rate the program from 0 (none) to 5 (high).

- Rate the program 0 or 1 if it contains little or none of the behavior in that category.

[1] Used with permission of The National Institute on Media and the Family.

- Rate the program 2 or 3 if it contains a moderate amount of the behavior in that category.
- Rate the program 4 or 5 if it contains a high amount of the behavior in that category.

Circle the number that best fits the amount of violence or other behaviors you are seeing.

You'll see that there are two violence ratings—the first includes physical and verbal violence. Physical violence includes hitting, kicking, slapping, tripping, knocking someone over, throwing something, violence with weapons, and so on. Verbal violence includes put-downs, name calling, using foul language, screaming, racial slurs, yelling in a threatening manner.

The second category has you rate the program's use of violence. Was the level of violence necessary for the plot of the show or was it just there to shock the viewer?

Television Program: _____
Industry Rating: _____
(TVY, TVY7, TV-Y7-FV, TVG, TVPG, TV14, TVMA)

Violence: Action or words intended to hurt someone or something.

None	Low				High
GO—GO——CAUTION——CAUTION——STOP——STOP					
0	1	2	3	4	5

Violence Portrayal: A lower score on this scale means that, if there is violence, it is necessary for the story and is not exaggerated.

None	Low			High	
GO—GO—CAUTION——CAUTION——STOP—STOP					
0	1	2	3	4	5

Fear: Contains scenes that cause fear in children.

None	Low			High	
GO—GO—CAUTION——CAUTION——STOP—STOP					
0	1	2	3	4	5

Illegal/Harmful: Contains scenes with behaviors that would be illegal or dangerous for kids to imitate.

None	Low			High	
GO—GO—CAUTION——CAUTION——STOP—STOP					
0	1	2	3	4	5

Language: Contains course, obscene, sexually suggestive, explicit, or disrespectful language.

None	Low			High	
GO—GO—CAUTION——CAUTION——STOP—STOP					
0	1	2	3	4	5

Nudity: Contains provocative scenes.

None	Low			High	
GO—GO—CAUTION——CAUTION——STOP—STOP					
0	1	2	3	4	5

Sexual Content: Contains portrayals of sexual behavior.

None	Low				High
GO	GO	CAUTION	CAUTION	STOP	STOP
0	1	2	3	4	5

Congratulations! You have now joined the thousands of parents who have been using KidScore to take a closer look at the media their children are viewing.

Now you need to decide what age group this show is best suited (or not suited) for.

If your show rated all 0's and 1's (GO) then it will be suited for all children. (Remember, however, that shows made especially for children are best suited for ages 3–7.)

If your show rated all 4's and 5's (STOP) then it is probably not suited for any age child.

If your show rated a mixture of GO—CAUTION—STOP scores then you need to evaluate the show based on your values, knowledge of your child, and his or her age. The younger the child, the more careful you should be with shows that fall in the "Stop" or "Caution" category. Always talk with your child about what they are watching.

How would you rate this show for these age categories?

• • • • • • • • • • •

	GO	CAUTION	STOP
3–7			
8–12			
13–17			
Your Child			

Do you agree with the rating the industry gave this show?

Activity: What to Do?

For parents and children ages three to twelve.

One of the most common reasons we turn on the television is because we are bored. The TV is turned on as a first reaction to "What do I do now?" Children can easily fall into this behavior pattern.

Sometimes, children need a little help to spark their own creativity. There are many suggestions in this book, and references to other sources which can help provide this spark. The following is an activity you may want to try to get you started.

Tell your child that you want to make a family list of things to do for fun when homework and jobs are finished. Have everyone contribute to the list. (Hint: Activities cannot include TV, video, or computer games.)

- Some children like to make their own list in a little notebook they can keep handy.

• • • • • • • • • • •

- Other families tape their activity list on the wall or refrigerator.
- Cut the list apart so that each idea is on its own slip of paper. Put the slips into a jar or box and draw an activity at random as opportunities present themselves. (Younger children might want to decorate the box.)

Creating a list helps children see they really have choices other than TV. For parents it is helpful to direct kids to a list rather than come up with ideas every time the kids complain, "I'm bored!"

One parent had the idea that if the child couldn't find an activity from the Things to Do jar, then they could always choose from the Job jar. This has a way of sparking children's creativity.

If they can't find anything to do, sometimes kids *are* just bored. Learning how to deal with boredom is one of the things kids must learn. A parent's quick fix or turning on the TV or video game short circuits this valuable learning experience. Children are highly creative and most of the time "I'm bored" turns into a fun and creative project.

The following books are full of ideas for activities that provide alternatives to TV.

1. *The Baby Games: The Joyful Guide to Child's Play from Birth to Three Years*
   by Elaine Martin, 1988
2. *Child's Play: 200 Instant Crafts and Activities for Preschoolers*
   by Leslie Hamilton, 1989

● ● ● ● ● ● ● ● ● ● ●

3. 300 *Three Minute Games: Quick and Easy Activities of 2–5 Year Olds*
   by Jackie Silberg, illustrated by Cheryl Kirk Noll, 1997
4. 365 *TV-Free Activities You Do With Your Child*
   by Steven J. Bennett, Ruth Bennett, 1996
5. *Day by Day Activity Book: 365 Days of Fun Ideas for Parents, Teachers & Kids*
   by Susan Ohanian, 1997
6. 365 *Afterschool Activities: TV-Free Fun for Kids 7–12*
   by Sheila Ellison, Judith Anne Gray, 1995
7. 365 *Outdoor Activities You Can Do With Your Child*
   by Steven J. Bennett, Ruth Bennett, 1993

Activity: TV Parental Guidelines and the V-Chip

For parents.

The TV Parental Guidelines were devised by the television industry to provide parents with a rating system to help them choose suitable programs for their children to view.

These guidelines also work with the V-chip, which is available on all new televisions larger than thirteen inches. The V-chip is a device that allows parents to program their television to block the reception of programs with ratings they would find inappropriate for their child.

● ● ● ● ● ● ● ● ● ● ●

You can find a show's Parental Guideline rating by looking in your daily newspaper or TV guide. Also, the guideline is always broadcast at the beginning of each show. (News programs and sports shows do not carry a guideline.)

List five of your children's favorite television shows. How are they rated? Record each show's Parental Guideline rating. Guidelines are explained below.

Television Show   **Parental Guideline Rating**

1. _____   _____

2. _____   _____

3. _____   _____

4. _____   _____

5. _____   _____

Two guideline categories are designed for shows directed at children:

TVY All Children: This program has been deemed by the industry rating board as acceptable for all children, including those from ages two to six. Includes animated and live action.

TVY7 Directed to Older Children: For children ages seven or above. These programs may include elements of mild fantasy violence, comedic violence, or may frighten those children under the age of seven. If the program contains more intense fantasy violence, it will be labeled TV-Y7-FV.

Four guideline categories are designed for programs aimed at everyone (not specifically designed for children).

TVG General Audience: These programs, although not designed for children, are deemed to contain little or no violence, strong language, or sexual dialogue or situations. Material is appropriate for people of all ages.

TVPG Parental Guidance Suggested: These programs contain material that some parents might find unsuitable for younger children. The program will be labeled and contains some elements of

- moderate violence (V)
- some sexual situations (S)

- infrequent coarse language (L)
- some suggestive dialogue (D)

TV14 Parents Strongly Cautioned: These programs contain elements of
- intense violence (V)
- intense sexual situations (S)
- strong, coarse language (L)
- intensely suggestive language (D)

Many parents would find these elements unsuitable for children under the age of fourteen, and are urged to monitor these programs and use caution in judging whether these programs are suitable for viewing.

TVMA Mature Audience Only: These programs are deemed suitable only for viewers seventeen and older and contain:
- graphic violence (V)
- explicit sexual activity (S)
- crude, indecent language (L)

There is also one more program designation, **E/I:** These are educational/informational programs. Many have themes that would be of interest to children.

Remember: These guidelines are only guidelines. Parents need to closely monitor the programs children are watching. Individual shows may contain elements that you find objectionable, no matter what their industry rating, or you may find that watching the program with your child gives you a chance to talk about difficult themes.

Activity: Healthy Media Use: TV Plan

For parents.

Healthy television use is more important than ever in today's media-saturated world. Television is usually the most frequently used form of media in the house. Setting guidelines for its use is important. The younger your child is (ages seven and under) the more important it is that you, as parent, decide what is okay for TV viewing.

As your child gets older (ages eight to twelve), it is important to set guidelines that allow for more input and choice. As parent, you can set rules on amount of viewing, when, and types of shows.

It is still important with teenagers to have TV guidelines. In reality, teens usually watch the least amount of TV because they get more interested in music and are often involved in sports and other school activities.

Check off the TV Plan actions that address some of the concerns you have about your children's television use, or that fit your family's needs for healthy media use.

Choose one or two of those you checked that you feel you can start right away. Write them down. At the end of the week, check off if you started that action step.

As you are successful with an action step, add another one to your TV Plan until you have actions in place that ensure your family's healthy media use of television.

The action steps have been divided into two categories. The first category helps to set guidelines for the amount of television viewed. The second category focuses on the content of television. You might choose action steps from one or both categories, depending on your family's needs. Perhaps you already have rules about the amount of television viewing, but are concerned about the kinds of programs. Choose an action from the second category. You will find that some action steps are in both categories.

FAMILY TV PLAN

Amount of TV viewed

___ *Avoid using television as a baby-sitter.*
Think of how careful you are about choosing a baby-sitter and daycare. Try to be just as careful about what your children watch on TV every day.

___ *Keep televisions out of kids' bedrooms.*
It is difficult to monitor what your child is watching when they are watching TV in their own room. Having a television in a child's room discourages participation in family activities and encourages them to watch TV when they could be studying, reading, or sleeping.

___ *Set some guidelines about when and what children watch.*
This can be done in conversation with your children, but the final call belongs to the adults. The clearer the rules the better.
 • No TV before school
 • No TV until homework is completed

Setting new limits may be upsetting to your children at first, but consistency is very important.

Limit time that can be spent watching television.

___ *Practice appointment television. Decide in advance what's good and watch it as a family.*

Go through the TV listings in the paper on Sunday and make family decisions on shows to watch for the week.

- Make a weekly schedule of what shows to watch.
- Urge kids to use the TV listings to find shows to watch. This cuts down on impulse use of television.

Discuss reasons for the decisions with your children. If in doubt, get more information. In choosing television shows or videos, make use of independent evaluations, like KidScore, television and movie guides, articles in magazines, etc. Discuss issues and ideas with other adults, friends, and parents of your children's playmates.

- Decide whether to have no television for children under two years of age.

___ *Turn TV off during meals.*

Catch up with one another. Focus on each other. Share stories and activities from each family member's day.

___ *Put the family on a TV diet.*

Schedule some fun alternative activities. When you do watch television, watch it with your children. If no one is watching the television set, turn it off.

___ *Create a TV coupon system.*

Kids get a set number of coupons each week and turn them in when they watch a program. Each coupon is worth one-half hour of television time. Unused coupons can be cashed in for a special family activity.

___ *Don't make the TV the focal point of the room.*
Make your children the focus of your attention, not the television. Research shows that people watch less TV if it is not in the most prominent location in the room.

CONTENT OF TV PROGRAMS

___ *Know what your kids are watching.*
It is important to be aware of program content as well as the content of the daily news. The younger the child, the more impressionable he or she is, and the less experienced in evaluating content against the values of family and community. Additionally, emotional images may intrude upon and interrupt sleep.
- When possible view programs together.
- If you own a new TV, investigate using the V-chip to help you filter out unacceptable programs for your child.

___ *Talk to your child about what he or she is watching.*
Discuss what you are watching and ask specific questions. Ask what they see, as it may be very different from what you see. Ask them to tell you what things mean to them. Ask them why they watch specific shows, what characters they like and don't like. Discuss the commercials and their perception of toys, cereals, and so on, and the people who sell them.

___ *Use the VCR to your advantage.*

Tape a good show and schedule a special family viewing—complete with popcorn. If a show is on at an inconvenient time such as mealtime, homework time, or family time, tape it to watch later. Videotape TV shows for your child, so they have a backup when there is nothing appropriate on the television for them to watch.

___ *Patronize good programs and demand more of them.*

Express your opinions to television and radio stations, network executives, and advertisers. Tell them not only what you do not like, but also what you do like. Addresses for networks and local stations are in your TV listings. Also, remember that your money has a voice of its own.

Activity: TV Plan

For parents.

You have spent a lot of time evaluating your family's television viewing habits and are now ready to make a TV Plan. Having guidelines for healthy television viewing is a big step in shaping your child's cyberhood.

Write down the one or two actions from the previous activity that you feel you can start this week. After one week, check off if you have started that action step. If you are successful, add another action until you have a TV plan in place that promotes your family's healthy media use.

Action Steps: **Week 1**

1. _____   _____

     _____   _____

2. _____   _____

     _____   _____

3. _____   _____

     _____   _____

4. _____   _____

     _____   _____

5. _____   _____

     _____   _____

6. _____   _____

     _____   _____

7. _____   _____

     _____   _____

8. _____   _____

     _____   _____

9. _____   _____

     _____   _____

10. _____   _____

     _____   _____

The job of sorting out the pros and cons of programming can seem overwhelming. You may just have a mind to toss out the TV and be done with it altogether. However, your children will eventually watch somewhere else. So, you're left with one option, the same one you'll find throughout this book: Get involved. You're already on your way to becoming a critical viewer. You can help your children become critical viewers, too. Watch with them whenever you can, and engage them in discussions about what they see and hear. Ask questions, offer opinions, be ready to talk. Help them identify the messages being communicated in their favorite shows. Help them discover their own opinions about what TV has to say. In the process, you'll be helping them develop the ability to think for themselves. The value of that goes far beyond becoming an informed viewer and developing healthier TV habits.

CHAPTER FIVE

• • • • • • • • • •

Infotainment: Kids and the News

"All the news that's fit to print," declares the decades-old mission statement of the *New York Times.* It's as much a promise of integrity as a goal to live up to. It's the kind of thinking that set standards for journalism, the kind of thinking that went largely unchallenged by the best newspapers for most of this century. Then came television. And, in just a few decades, its power bloomed. Now, television is setting new standards for reporting the news and, for print media, this captivating electronic medium is a hard act to follow. Many newspapers are loosening the reins on hard journalism to compete with what television news has to offer. And what it offers has more and more to do with arousing our emotions and keeping us watching—like programming in general. Its information-dispensing advantages aside, no one needs to be reminded that TV news serves up generous helpings of violence, scandal, and tragedy. When our kids are around, we have to think twice before turning on the TV to see what's going on in the world. We want to spare them the inevitable parade of horrors, stay the perception that the world is a terrible place. A generation ago news was, for the most part, just news; not always pleasant, of course, but reliably straightforward, uneditorialized reporting of newsworthy events and information. Now we have electrifying human dramas delivered with tantalizing candor, in gratuitous detail. Real-life atrocities with little value other than to shock. Near miniseries scandals of celebrity murders and philandering politicians. In short, our news looks very much like prime-time entertainment.

• • • • • • • • •

The average daily edition of the *New York Times* contains more information than the average person was exposed to in a lifetime at the time of the American Revolution.

• • • • • • • • •

Every parent of school-age children faces the effects of this powerful breed of news. Whether or not you turn on the TV, your kids are going to get the news—at school, from friends, on the radio, in tabloid headlines at the grocery store. The Clinton-Lewinsky scandal of 1998 fueled the issue for many families across the United States. With their hunger for inglorious detail and typical lack of restraint, the networks put the seamiest of stories into the hands of children—and parents are forced to deal with the consequences.

How stories like this are covered is a phenomenon in itself. Taking the lead from successful mainstream TV, reporting crimes, tragedies, and scandal has become big business. Arousing our emotions and getting our attention is profitable, so more and more news stories are reported in entertainment-like fashion. Emotional jolts and technical tricks work just as well in the news as in television dramas. Nowhere is this more evident than in crime reporting. With the help of roving helicopters, Los Angeles stations are making the most of the trend toward *infotainment,* boldly filming shootings, murders, suicides, and other violent crimes *live* every night. The candid footage is edited down to the critical punches and shown on the nightly news. These stations are living up to the age-old rule of cheap journalism: "If it bleeds, it leads." Thankfully, the prevalence of tall buildings in other large cities, like San Francisco or New York, make this aerial-driven coverage difficult to emulate.

Besides arousing our emotions and earning our viewership, crime coverage is popular for two other reasons. First, it's easy to cover and, therefore, relatively inexpensive for producers. Not much investigation goes into reporting a crime. Crime speaks for itself, and reporting it is a formula job: pictures of the crime scene, shots and interviews with the top-ranking officer on the scene, relatives, witnesses, and neighbors. Second, stations gravitate toward crime reporting and other kinds of human tragedy for the simple reason that pictures speak louder than words. Because television is a picture-based rather than language-based medium, news has a built-in bias toward events which lend themselves to pictures. If it isn't pictureworthy, it isn't likely to get covered. So, we see lots of car accidents, gun crimes, burning buildings, and hurricane-swept homes. We see less about abstract (and truly newsworthy) issues like education, the environment, poverty, the arts, science, labor, and international relations. With the excess of mayhem in the news we become conditioned to seeing and hearing about crime, violence, and tragedy. After a while, we cease to be aroused. So, like programming, news needs to up the ante in order to keep us watching.

Holding your attention is so important that the decision about *what* to report about a given story becomes critical. Let's say that you're watching a story about a crime in your neighborhood. You see the formulaic coverage unfold—crime scene shots, candid interviews, reporter commentary. The featured witness gives a highly emotional response to the crime, such as, "That's it, I'm moving out." You might easily draw the conclusion that this reaction is typical of neighborhood sentiment as a whole. But what you don't know is that the witness is one of three actually interviewed about the crime; the other two reactions were, in fact, moderate. However, moderate doesn't get you hooked. Emotionally arousing wins every

> The average length of a TV news story is forty seconds

time. So, you can see how what is and is not covered in the news can lead to misconceptions. If your local news is predominantly filled with crime stories (as many local broadcasts are), you might easily perceive your community to be riddled with crime. Studies have shown that because crime is over-covered on television news, the more people watch the news on TV, the more they overestimate crime rates. While crime rates are in fact declining nationwide, the local news usually paints a very different picture.

Every year, the Rocky Mountain Media Watch (RMMW) analyzes news on national and local levels. Their most recent survey led to the conclusion that "the news is seriously and consistently out of balance on most stations, with a heavy emphasis on crime, disaster, hype, triviality, and commercials." Late-breaking crimes and personal misfortunes have become the news of the day. According to the findings, nearly 40 percent of news, on average, is about crime and disaster. Twenty-five percent is given to *fluff*—on-air chit-chat between anchors, promotions and previews of upcoming stories, and trivial items like celebrity news. News about health, government, and the economy each average almost 10 percent. With news like this, it's easy to understand how kids can develop a distorted view of the world.

RMMW found imbalances in other aspects of the news that are worth considering in light of the fact that children are watching. Studies revealed that 75 percent of all anchors, including weather and sports hosts, are men; so are 70 percent of the experts, authorities, and sources whose opinions are given airtime on newscasts. In news stories themselves, women outnumber men as victims, and ethnic minorities appear frequently around crime events as both perpetrators and victims.

With more and more news becoming less newsworthy, the line between news and entertainment is blurring. In 1993, while doing research for another book, I met a TV producer who predicted that we would be watching death for entertain-

ment by the end of the century. I didn't put his speculation in
the book because I thought it was too extreme. Well, if you've
ever watched one of the new reality shows, you know his prediction has been proven true. Shows like *Real TV* and *The
World's Wildest Police Videos* offer
real-life tragedy and death packaged to look newslike—and clearly
geared to entertain. They feature
real footage, often intercut with
comments from witnesses, relatives, police officers, and rescue
personnel. Morally one notch

In 1968, the average length of
a sound bite on TV news was
42.3 seconds. By 1992, it had
shrunk to 8.2 seconds.

lower than fictional TV stories of tragedy and death, these programs feature the real thing in grisly detail. We see cars
wrapped around poles and *real* passengers thrown to *real*
deaths, *real* people falling from *real* cliffs, and being mauled
by *real* wild animals. The newslike format is supposed to suggest we're getting something valuable, like insight into real life
events. Of course, this isn't news, or even information. Besides, made-up TV tragedy is bad enough; do we have to see it
for real? Our kids already have a hard time taking pain, misery,
and, even death, seriously, thanks to the glut of violence in entertainment media. They're already becoming desensitized to
what *isn't* real. The same fate applies to reality shows. To keep
ahead of our inevitable apathy, these programs must become
more and more extreme. They must compete with each other
for real human tragedy, the same way the Los Angeles stations
compete for live crime.

Just as programming is driven to deliver eyeballs to advertisers, news departments are driven by the economics of viewership. Stations have to bring in viewers in order to compete.
The advent of twenty-four-hour news channels like CNN and
Fox News has put much greater competitive pressure on the
networks. In order to pick up viewer interest around the clock,
these stations have to fill up the time with interesting material. So, tragedy is played up and story content becomes more

outrageous. Sadly, the best thing that happened to CNN's ratings in 1997 was the death of Princess Diana. In 1999, it was the fatal plane crash of John F. Kennedy, Jr. Given the public's penchant for tragedy, here was an event that could provide lots of mileage for an able network. If you're paying attention, you'll see more sensationalized stories in the news during the annual ratings sweeps in November, February, and May.

News magazines like *20/20, 48 Hours,* and *Dateline NBC* are another extension of network competition. And, in the new tradition of entertainment news, they, too, are helping to blur the line between news and entertainment. On one hand, many news magazines are hosted by respected news anchors, such as Diane Sawyer and Dan Rather, and produced using news-style reporting and candid interviews; all of this lends an air of credibility to the news magazine agenda. On the other hand, most of the storylines for these programs are chosen not because they are newsworthy but because they are entertaining. So, we have what looks like news, but feels more like entertainment.

More than 50 percent of children surveyed said they felt "angry, sad, or depressed" after watching the TV news. (*Children Now,* 1994.)

Bona fide news programs, like the *McLaughlin Group* and *Crossfire,* derive their legitimacy not only from the news-oriented issues they present, but also from journalists and other pundits they invite as regular guests. Underlying all this credibility is the basic need to attract viewers. Typically, these shows revolve around a moderator and one or more guests who deliberate varying perspectives on a given issue. The moderator baits the guests to keep the controversy in play, which adds an element of entertainment for viewers. A journalistic version of a food fight is often the result.

Journalists are even making appearances as themselves in movies. Since movies are eventually run on television, this means you can see a journalist on the news and an hour later *playing* the role for entertainment. And, so, the line softens a little more.

While the news business makes no apologies for passing off surefire attention getters as news, neither does it feel the need to let you in on one of its sneakiest secrets: the video news release, or VNR. Essentially, a VNR is a pre-edited, pre-scripted news package that channels can pick up free via satellite, and broadcast as part of their programming. What most viewers don't realize is that these newslike segments are actually advertisements. VNRs are produced by corporations to promote an agenda. They're infomercials done documentary-style, and the quality is very good. As you watch the evening news, you might see a three-minute VNR clip without realizing it's an ad. Nowhere in the segment is the name of the sponsoring company mentioned. Nor are you told that the station or network didn't produce it. The beauty of a VNR is that it can slip right into a regular newscast as though it belonged.

Often VNRs are used to promote health products, environmental issues, and political campaigns. While VNRs don't actually lie to you, they are very cagey in delivering their message. For example, a lumber company might produce a VNR which talks about the varieties of wildlife attracted to a new-growth forest. Remember, you don't know that a lumber company produced the segment you are watching, so it seems like a good piece of science reporting. Of course, what's really going on is a subtle effort to influence your attitude about timber harvesting. The underlying message is that cutting down trees paves the way for good things. Since, for now, there are no regulations requiring VNRs to be identified as such, all of us are challenged to be more critical viewers, to accept nothing at face value.

That goes for local news, too. Local news stations have everything at stake where viewership is concerned; because local news is the only thing left that local stations produce themselves, news is how they compete in a local market. Of course, news for news' sake doesn't woo viewers. So, flashy sets and attractive anchors, scripted camaraderie, and strategic storylines are choreographed to make news more entertaining. Because we tend to identify with our local channel, local stations work hard to establish a relationship between us and the anchors. If they do a good job, the *home channel phenomenon* will kick in: We'll begin watching their channel to get the news. Even if we surf, chances are we'll return to home base.

Since news is a fact of life, and *real* news is essential to maintaining an informed perspective, what's a parent to do? You can keep younger children from watching the news altogether, but older kids are going to watch. So, you need to help them become critical viewers, just as with regular programming. You need to redefine for them the line between news and entertainment. By watching with your kids whenever possible and initiating discussions of news content—for better *and* worse—you can help them learn the difference between hard news and soft. You can also help them differentiate between fantasy and reality, a skill sorely lacking in a generation of kids raised on advertising. Although television isn't likely to take a stand for "all the news that's fit to watch," at least we can teach our children to make the distinction themselves. The following activities should help you and your children become more discriminating consumers of TV news.

• • • • • • • •

Channel One is the current-events TV news program that 8 million students watch in school. The twelve-minute daily program includes two minutes of commercials. The students in the participating schools are *required* to watch the commercials.

• • • • • • • •

CHAPTER FIVE ACTIVITIES

Activity: Where's the News?

For parents and children ages eight and older.

The world of information has exploded. Many times we feel we are on overload from all the information sent our way. But our view of our community, our country, and the world is greatly shaped by the news stories we hear, see, and read. So where do we get our news? Where do our children get the news?

Child or teen: Think of recent news stories, circle in orange where your news comes from.

Parent: Circle in blue where your news comes from.

If your child is under ten years old, think of news as the stories we hear about what is happening in our neighborhood, our city, country, and the world. Think perhaps of a major news story that has recently happened. Ask your child if they have heard about this story and, then, where they heard about it.

Radio	Friends	Headlines	Fax
Channel One	Television News	Newspaper	MTV
School	Internet	Magazines	Co-workers
Advertising	Newsletters/Fliers	Late Night Talk Shows	Pagers

Activity: The New News

For parents and children ages ten and older.

Find out if your favorite local newscast has developed into the new news. How often does your news show slip from news into entertainment?

Choose your favorite half-hour local evening news program.

As you watch, circle as many items below that indicate your news program is crossing the line into entertainment.

Theme songs   Attractive model-type anchors   Hype

Fancy set   Joking between anchors   Entertainment news stories

High impact visuals   Virtual sets   Prize giveaways

3-D weather maps   Live remote transmissions

Here are some questions about newscasts that you can discuss with your children:

- What is the purpose of a newscast?
- Do the add-ons make news more informative?
- Are you viewing more news or more entertainment?
- Does a story add to your knowledge of an issue, your community, or the world, or does it just make you feel good?

- Are the news stories giving you all the information you need?
- With a stopwatch, time each news story and record its length.
- Are the news stories longer or shorter than forty seconds? How does the length of a news story affect the information you are receiving?

Activity: Rate Your News

For parents and children ages ten and older.

As the line between news and entertainment continues to blur, it's more important than ever to be able to recognize the difference. The pressure for ratings on local newscasts is high. They must have high ratings to attract advertising and, thus, turn a profit. How can you judge whether your local station is providing your community with news that will improve the quality of life in your hometown? Here are some questions you can ask each other as you watch local news programs. They will help your child begin to see the difference between entertainment and news, and ratings hype and real information.

Watch and compare several local news stations, and ask these questions while you view each news show.

See which stations are giving you infotainment and which are giving you credible news.

● ● ● ● ● ● ● ● ● ● ●

CHANNEL_____	RED	GREEN
1. Does the program start with sensational crime leaders?	YES	NO
2. Does the program show sensational footage that is not really important?	YES	NO
3. Does the station cover what is really important in your community?	NO	YES
4. Do the news stories make you think, not just feel?	NO	YES
5. Do the news stories needlessly prey on victim's emotions? (i.e., Ask a mother how she feels about her child's sudden death? Do they push microphones in people's faces?)	YES	NO
6. Do the news anchors engage in a lot of trivial chit-chat?	YES	NO
7. Does the news show go in depth with longer stories on important issues?	NO	YES
8. Does the news station often make news out of upcoming movies or television specials?	YES	NO
9. Does the station regularly report on a range of topics, covering all members of your community?	NO	YES

If many of your answers fall in the Green column, then your local news is on track, reporting real news. If many of

● ● ● ● ● ● ● ● ● ● ●

your answers fall in the Red column, than perhaps your local news is offering more infotainment than news.

If you feel your news station is airing more infotainment than news, call and complain. When you feel they are doing a good job reporting news that is important in your community, call them and let them know.

CHAPTER SIX

• • • • • • • • • •

Media Advertising

As we have seen, the business model behind most media is built on delivering audiences to advertisers. Media and advertising, then, are joined at the hip. Media need advertisers to pay the bills, and advertisers need media as the vehicle for their messages. No advertisers, no media. So, we can't completely understand media without also understanding advertising.

Whenever I get into a discussion of advertising and how it works I can't help but recall a television ad I watched a few years ago with my daughter. It so clearly illustrates the psychology of advertising and the goal of all those advertising bucks. Erin and I were settled into the couch enjoying a program together, when it came time for the inevitable commercial break. One of the ads that came on was new to both of us. We watched as a series of charming, nostalgic images followed one after another: a horsedrawn sleigh in a snow-covered field, a house on hill, a wreath on the door, friendly faces exchanging gifts before a fire, a Christmas tree sparkling in the background. Twenty seconds into this thirty-second spot, we still had no idea what product was being sold. My daughter guessed that the mystery product would turn out to be beer; my money was on Hallmark. We were both wrong. The commercial closed with a majestic shot of a jet against an azure sky and cottony clouds. The voiceover said: "American Airlines. Bringing friends together for the holidays." How about that, an airline ad. Who could have known? No matter. What was important was that we felt good about American Airlines (for the moment, anyway). What a wonderful company to bring people together at such a special time. Just the response the advertiser had in mind. American Airlines didn't spend its money boasting an impressive safety record, state-of the-art aircraft, or a professional staff. The truth is, feelings—not facts—sell. The ad could just as well have been for beer or greeting cards if it got us to *feel* the right way.

Getting us to respond a certain way is the tried and true MO of the advertising industry: First, an ad creates a desired emotional state, then it links a product or message to that state. Emotions are so powerful that critical thinking has no place in advertising, indeed, it could be a death knell. If we think too much, we might not buy. Good advertisements get us to feel first, and think little, if at all. Messages geared to create an emotional response sneak in under the radar of critical thinking and judgment. My daughter and I watched two-thirds of a new ad before we realized what was being sold. The advertiser is using that time to create just the right emotional state that will make you feel good about a product or message, create a desire for the product, or align the advertiser's promise with your needs. By employing emotional hotbuttons, advertisers are trying to open you up and get inside. They appeal to emotional needs like belonging, feeling attractive, and feeling rewarded.

The emotion they inspire in us doesn't have to be pleasant in order to be effective. Consider an ad for a home security system: You watch an intruder creeping around a house at night, breaking a window, then climbing inside. The next shot shows a sleeping child, followed by a parent waking with a start—your imagination has no problem embellishing along the way. Just when you're scared enough, enters the hero: the

A to Z Home Security System. You can't help but look at the product favorably. In fact, the advertiser hopes that you'll be convinced you really *need* that home security system.

In the process of creating an emotional state, advertisers are also doing something else. They're working hard to shape attitudes and values, because attitudes and values motivate behavior. When the goal is to get you to buy something, influencing behavior is essential. To really influence your decision to buy, an advertiser has to inspire you to change your behavior, to switch from brand X to brand Y, to wear a particular brand of jeans, to drink only one soft drink. To get you to act a certain way, advertisers need to make their attitudes your attitudes, its values your values. Although it's hard to admit, they're very successful at doing just that.

The ads we see on TV and in other forms of media are highly produced. Proportionally, more time, money, and resources go into producing one thirty-second commercial than into any program we might watch on television. Just thirty seconds of advertising can take months to create. Every element is designed, analyzed, massaged, tweaked, and integrated to meet specific goals. Images, colors, textures, camera angles, lighting, sound, and music all come together to create the right emotional state and, at the same time, link a certain attitude or value to the product in a way that will influence behavior. Most ads have been tested and premarketed to ensure that the final product achieves the expected results. When an ad is finally released to the marketplace, it is repeated until it becomes familiar to us, comfortable, *right*.

The most powerful ad is the ad of which you're unaware. In fact, the ultimate goal of an advertiser is to influence you without you knowing it. Wait a minute, you might be thinking, you know an ad when you see one, right? However, ads today are so sophisticated and so entertaining that we find ourselves watching them just for fun. Super Bowl ads are a perfect example. Just because they're fun to watch doesn't mean they're not also doing their job. In fact, commonly, it's *because* an ad is fun that it's effective. If ads merely amounted to spectacle and entertainment, advertisers wouldn't dump billions of dollars into producing them.

An ad may entertain you, you may realize what it's trying to sell, but chances are it's also influencing how you feel about the product or message it promotes. Remember, getting you to a particular emotional state is how an ad says "Open sesame." Even if you *always* view advertising with a critical eye and manage to avoid its influence, there are enough of us who don't to keep advertisers hard at work. In 1997, it was estimated that 223 billion dollars were spent on TV, cable, radio, newspaper, and magazine advertising.

> The amount spent on electronic media advertising in 1999 exceeded $132 billion.

With all that money at work—not to mention creativity, strategizing, and technology—it's no surprise that advertising teaches values better than anything else. And, as you know by now, there's no shortage of media vehicles to do the job—television, movies, videos, video games, the Internet, radio, and countless print opportunities. Our children can't help but be exposed to advertising, and the value messages it promotes. Children today are getting most of their information about what's important from entities whose goal is to sell them something, rather than from the old cornerstones of values education: family, school, and religion. When you consider that the typical six year old *doesn't* know an ad when he or she sees one, *can't* distinguish between an ad trying to sell and a program that entertains, and *can't* separate fantasy from reality, you begin to realize the power advertising wields. One recent study found that when young children were asked who they would believe—their parents telling them something was true or a TV character (even an animated one) telling them the opposite was true—70 percent said they would believe what the TV character told them. While adults have the capacity to be more jaded about the advertising messages they see, kids are a clean slate and the perfect audience for advertisers' strategic messages.

• • • • • • • •

Children see approximately twenty thousand ads each year on TV alone.

• • • • • • • •

The latest advertising medium with which parents must contend is the Internet. World Wide Web pages now send advertisements to people around the globe. While commercial websites were nonexistent as recently as 1993, today they are uncountable. In true Internet form, online advertising is currently unregulated, free to evolve unhindered and unchecked. So, the rush is on for advertisers to attract and interact with kids online before regulations prevent them from doing so.

Branded play environments have been among the hottest trends in Internet advertising. In many of these colorful, entertaining websites, marketers have used prizes, games, and animated characters to collect data from, and sell products to, children as young as four. Given what we know of the cyberspace explosion of covert data collection and selling of personal profiles to third parties (chapter 7), this invasion of privacy is a frightening prospect for parents. Laws that went into effect in the year 2000 limit some data collection activities, but there is no limit on what some branded sites can do in blurring the line between entertainment and advertising. Crayola, for example, has an activity-based site that enables kids to print out drawings to color in, paint, or cut out. Of course, kids can't complete the activity without Crayola tools. In essence, the ad and the site are so interwoven that a child can't tell them apart. While Crayola is providing kids with an opportunity for fun—which isn't a bad thing—it also wants to sell products, which, at the very least, is something to be aware of. Until the Federal Trade Commission establishes rules and regulations about what advertisers can and cannot do on the Internet, parents have reason to be concerned about where this road will take their children.

There's every reason to pay attention to advertising's interest in your kids—not just because advertising is about manipulating emotions and shaping values for their own purposes but, because, increasingly, advertising specifically targets children. In the words of the famous bank robber, Willie Sutton, "that's where the money is," and advertisers know it. Of course, Sutton was referring to banks but, for advertisers, kids are consumers they can bank on. More and more, children *are* where the money is. Like Sutton, who returned to robbing banks every chance he got, advertisers aren't likely to ignore the youth market—it's hard to turn away from a sure thing.

With many double-income families and more single working parents today, moms and dads have less time to supervise their kids' purchasing choices and, often, feel pressed to keep them occupied. Increasingly, parents are likely to give their children money to buy things on their own. As a result, kids are taking a more active role in shopping and purchasing decisions, which means they're gaining more of the purchasing power. It's estimated that kids eighteen and younger spend about fifty billion dollars a year. Although that's an impressive figure, it's nothing compared to where the real money is—not in their purchasing power, but in their purchasing *influence*. You know it as the *nag factor*: "We have to have this one, Mom, it's the coolest," "Everyone's getting 'em, Dad, can't we *pleease?*" The purchasing influence of kids today is estimated to be ten times greater than their purchasing power: about 500 billion dollars a year. And this figure is increasing by 20 percent annually.

Media Advertising Myths and Facts

Myth: Young children can recognize commercials.

Fact: Young children do not know the difference between commercials and programming. They do not understand that a commercial is trying to sell them something.

Myth: Mom and Dad make the family decisions.

Fact: Experts tell us that children control or influence over a half trillion dollars of consumer spending.

Myth: Liquor advertising is illegal on television.

Fact: It's not illegal. It was a voluntary agreement that liquor companies made in the 1930s. Seagrams broke the agreement in 1997, so we will be seeing more liquor ads on TV in the future.

Myth: Children's commercials are gender neutral for girls and boys.

Fact: Boys appear more often in commercials, even when the product is gender neutral. In the land of commercials, boys appear in more dominant roles, and are more active and aggressive. Girls are depicted as more submissive, shyer, and unlikely to assert themselves.

Myth: Children are savvy enough not to be influenced by commercials.

Fact: According to Consumer's Union, 30,000 commercial messages are targeted at American children each year, and their influence can be substantial.

Myth: Channel One is providing schools with free access to news and information programming as well as helping schools with their tight budgets.

Fact: According to the Center for Commercial Free Public Education, Channel One costs the taxpayers $1.8 billion per year in lost classroom time, which includes $300 million in class time allotted for the mandatory commercial watching.

So, advertisers have all the more reason to target kids with their advertisements. Like parents, they know all about the nag factor, and use it to their advantage. Advertisers know that even when kids may not have the money to buy, they often have a vote in the purchasing decision—that goes for products that have nothing to do with kids. Ford Explorer, for example, advertises in *Sports Illustrated for Kids*. Why? Because Ford counts on the likelihood that kids will cast votes when it comes time to choose the family car.

Advertisers also know that the nag factor works in more subtle ways. Take a trip to the grocery store, for instance. You cruise the aisles grabbing the products you need with your child in tow. You reach for a package of paper towels and your little one points to another brand and says, "No, get *that* kind." The price is about the same, so what do you care? Anyway, it'll probably prevent a scene, so you toss the other brand in the cart and get on with your shopping. On the surface, it all seems pretty innocent. Until you stop to wonder why a kid should have any interest in paper towels, much less a specific brand. The advertiser of those other paper towels knew just what they were doing when it aimed its ad at kids.

Advertising's quest to make a buck at the expense of children doesn't end there. Brand loyalty, the holy grail of advertising, also fuels their cause. The stated objective of advertisers industrywide is to establish brand loyalty by age *three*. And why not? They've proven it can be done, and the potential for greater returns is nearly a guarantee. So, advertisers bombard kids with skillfully produced persuasive messages about all kinds of products—if it can be pitched to a child, it will be. Studies show that children who watch the average number of hours of TV per week will see 20,000 ads in one year, and that's just on television. One study estimates that if you take into consideration all the advertising messages encountered in a day—on cereal boxes, signs, packages, TV, and radio—the average American child is exposed to 1.2 million advertising messages a year. Confronted with so many messages how can we *not* expect our children to be affected?

The abundance of advertising messages in media today drives advertisers to compete ever harder for our attention. They're always searching for ways to stand out and get their messages in front of us and in front of our children. One of the most controversial advertising efforts aimed at children today is a school-targeted program called Channel One. In nearly 13,000 U.S. schools, more than 8 million children watch this twelve-minute daily news program, which includes two minutes of commercials. Along with the daily program, Channel One provides participating schools with a television set for every class room. Not surprisingly, financially strapped school districts are particularly attracted to this offer. In return, a school district must sign an agreement making it mandatory for students to watch the two minutes of commercials aired with the program. The teachers have no choice. The students must pay attention to the commercials. Advertisers are happy to pay whopping fees for one of these thirty-second spots because they're assured a captive audience. Aside from the ethical question of advertising to children, critics denounce Channel One for encouraging poor nutrition by promoting soft drinks and candy, as well as for playing on children's insecurities in its efforts to sell products that will make them "popular."

> • • • • • • • •
> We have the undivided attention of millions of teenagers for 12 minutes a day. (Marketing brochure for Channel One.)
> • • • • • • • •

Similarly, shrinking educational funds have pushed school boards all over the country to open their doors to the influence of advertising, namely by seeking corporate help. Typically, in exchange for cash, companies are allowed to advertise their products on school rooftops, athletic scoreboards, sports uniforms, even on buses. The hallways of schools in one Colorado district are peppered with ads telling students that "M&Ms are better than straight As," and encouraging them to

"Satisfy your hunger for higher education with Snickers." At a high school in rural Georgia a student was suspended for wearing a Pepsi T-shirt on "Coke Day in the Schools." Students had been instructed to wear Coke shirts that day and spell out Coca-Cola on the school lawn to impress a visiting Coca-Cola executive. One lucky student was to win five hundred dollars from the soft drink giant.

Like the media it depends on to bring it to life, advertising is a prolific, permanent, and potent force in our culture. As with television, video games, the Internet, and the other media with which we live on a daily basis, you need to teach your kids how to think critically about advertising. You need to help them become *critical consumers*. By that, we mean that they should take nothing at face value, learn to ask questions, and *decode* what they see and hear in advertisements.

The place to start is by teaching your kids the first rule of thumb: An ad is trying to sell them something. The first question to ask is: *What is it trying to sell?* Then you can move on to helping them decide if the ad is truthful. Are things portrayed the way they are in real life? For example, is that toy really as big as the TV screen, or does it just look that way? Can a soft drink really make a person fly like a comet? Does a car really take off like a jet? You can teach older children to go a step further and ask themselves: Is the ad telling the whole story? For example, does the skateboarder in an ad perform without mistakes because his gear gives him superathletic ability, or because his falls were edited out?

Then, there are the impressions, illusions, and half-truths to contend with. This is where advertising can be very subtle and decoding more tricky. While laws prevent advertisers from telling outright lies, there are no rules against implied realities. For example, an ad that shows a teenage girl wearing a certain brand of jeans basking in the attentions of teenage boys is not only selling blue jeans, but implying that if you wear that brand you'll be popular. A cereal ad that shows a kid

laughing and happy as he eats a certain brand of cereal suggests that the cereal is responsible for his good mood.

As you begin the practice of decoding advertisements with
your kids don't limit your critiques to ads targeted at them. If
your kids are watching an ad, it's a good opportunity to open
discussion. Even ads that are meant to sell to adults can be appealing to kids simply because they're entertaining. Some beer
commercials, for example, feature animations and special effects no one could resist watching and, if ads like these can influence adults, why wouldn't they have the same effect on
children? By teaching your children to ask critical questions
you will help them understand how they are being manipulated and influenced. You will be teaching them to talk back to
advertisements. Once they get the hang of talking back to ads
they'll probably enjoy doing it. Advertising is one authority
they're allowed to buck.

Cyberhood Map

The following activities will help you educate your children
about techniques used in commercials and print ads to make
toys seem more appealing. The same techniques are used in
marketing cereals and other foods to children. They will discover that toys and other products that look great on TV may
not be that wonderful in real life.

Older children can learn to decode television commercials.
There's an activity to help them understand how commercials
encourage us to buy products or believe slogans. Finally,
schools are places where large numbers of children are a captive audience. This fact is not lost on advertisers, so, you need
to pay attention, too! More and more frequently, advertising is
finding its way into schools. What is happening in your
school? The last activity will help you make a careful assess-
ment of how far advertisers have reached into your child's
classroom.

CHAPTER SIX ACTIVITIES

Toys

For parents or parents with children ages five to twelve.

Many children's television shows are nothing more than half-hour commercials for toys. It's called *cross-marketing* when they link products with television shows and movies. Sometimes the shows, movies, or video games these toys are linked to are violent. The play they encourage mainly imitates what the child sees on the screen.

Survey the toys and other products you or your child own. How many are linked to television, movie, or video-game characters?

1. Check the toys that are linked to television, movies, video games:

_____ Action figures

_____ Dolls

_____ Animal figures

_____ Monster/space figures

_____ Dress up sets

_____ Guns/weapons

_____ Wrestling figures

_____ Action sets or props for action figures

2. Check other products you buy that are linked to media characters:

toothpaste ____   bed linen ____   foods ____

snacks ____   school supplies ____   utensils ____

clothes ____   shoes ____   hats ____

Make an effort to choose toys that encourage open-ended, creative play. These are toys that are longer lasting and will continue to be enjoyed by your child after the latest media character is history.

Some ideas are blocks, construction sets, play animals and insects, balls, clay, art materials, playhouse sets, puzzles, cars, trucks, airplanes, boats, tractors, dolls, family and community figures, dress up clothes, books, music, cards, and board games.

Activity: Toys and Advertising

For parents and children ages five through ten.

We've talked a lot about the different advertising techniques used to capture and hold our attention. Sometimes, it's helpful to step back and look at the whole ad and how that toy or food is made to appear to be just about the best thing you've ever seen. In real life, that toy may be a real disappointment, and that food won't make anyone want to sing or dance.

This activity will work best if you have the product or the toy available. Videotape or watch a commercial of a product or toy that you or your child owns. As you watch the commercial, try and pick out the differences in the toy (or product) as it appears in the commercial and as it is in real life.

Ask your child the following questions where they apply:

Does the toy seem bigger on TV? _____

Is the setting of the commercial a real home or is it a made-up environment? _____

Do the sounds the toy makes sound different on TV? _____

Is there exciting background music to the commercial that you don't have at home? _____

Is the toy pictured alone or is it grouped with a lot of other toys or ad-on equipment? _____

Can you actually play with the toy at home the same way its being played with in the ad? _____

Are you as happy when you play with this toy at home as the children on the television ad are? _____

Is the price of the toy or product mentioned? _____

Will owning this make you have more friends? _____

Activity: Magazine Advertising Collage

For parents and children ages eight and older.

Earlier, in chapter 3, we looked at television commercials and their use of emotional hot buttons and technical tricks to capture our attention. The advertising in print media grabs our attention with similar techniques. In this activity, you will make a collage of pictures that illustrate some of these advertising jolts and tricks.

Materials: magazines, scissors, paper, glue

Gather a collection of popular magazines, and cut out samples of advertisements. Spread these ads out in front of you and your child.

1. Choose ads that use some type of emotion to sell their products. Paste these pictures on a sheet of paper to make an advertising jolts collage.

   Can you find any ads that use these hot buttons to sell a product?

   violence   sex   humor   status   wealth

   fear   joy   sadness   happiness   adventure

   excitement   pride   pleasure   love

   Which hot buttons do advertisers appeal to most?

Ask your child:

- Will buying this product make you as happy as the people in the ad?
- Will you really have more fun just by eating a certain food or drinking a certain beverage?

2. Now, choose ads that use technical tricks to catch your eye. Paste these pictures on a larger sheet to make an advertising tricks collage.

   Can you find any ads that use these tricks to sell a product?

   intense color   special graphics

   enhanced picture of product   celebrities   slogans

   status images   glamorous background

   Which technique is used most often to sell a product?

Ask your child:

- Will buying an expensive pair of tennis shoes actually make you a super athlete?
- Will buying this product instantly solve real problems for you?
- Will that toy look the same in real life as it does in that ad?

   Ultimately, you don't want your children to be fooled by packaging or television ads for toys. They may look really great in that magazine ad or on TV, but may or may not be much fun in real life.

Activity: Decoding Television Commercials

For parents and children ages ten and older.

Besides the jolts and tricks discussed earlier, there are other techniques used in television commercials to activate our buying impulse. When we recognize and point these techniques out to children, they will learn to think more critically about what they see.

Videotape five or six commercials from your child's favorite program or a prime-time television show. Or watch a favorite television show with your child and see if you can spot any of the following techniques in the commercials. You will be looking for five different techniques. Familiarize yourself with each type, and talk to your child about them before you watch the tape or show. (If your child is younger than ten you may want to look for just one or two techniques.)

1. *Famous people.* This is a common technique. Movie stars or famous sports figures endorse a product or toy. The message here is that if this famous person likes this product, you will, too. Remind your kids that these people are being paid a lot of money for appearing in these commercials.

2. *Bandwagon.* Either through scenes (often of happy crowds) or statements (everyone/most people), we are told that lots and lots of people (usually por-

trayed as smart, cool, or rich) are using this product and that if we don't, we are missing the boat.

3. *Emotion.* Through pictures, music, or words this product is linked to feelings of joy, acceptance, excitement, happiness, or pride, or seems to help people in the ad avoid feelings of danger and fear.

4. *Links.* The product or toy is linked to a positive situation or activity. The message is that if you buy this product all the status, fun, excitement, or security that surrounds it in the commercial will be yours too.

5. *Empty words.* Many commercials use catchy slogans or product claims with empty words that are vague or don't really mean anything, i.e. "More doctors recommend . . ." or "Surveys show that . . ."

Which of these techniques can you spot in a commercial?

Write down what you and your child see.

1. Famous People _____

_____

2. Bandwagon _____

_____

3. Emotions _____

_____

4. Links _____

_____

5. Empty Words _____

_____

Activity: Advertising in Schools

For parents.

Schools are a captive market for advertisers to sell their products to kids. With school budgets stretched tighter, more and more school administrators are turning to advertising dollars to augment their school budgets. How much advertising is in your child's school? What do you think about it?

1. Keep an eye on the materials and giveaways your child brings home from school. Does your child carry around ads (for movies, cereal, candy, etc.) on their school supplies? Circle all that apply.

   Bookcovers   Pencils   Bookmarks

   Poster   Erasers   Books   Hats

   Stickers   Markers   Crayons

2. When you are in your child's school, take a look at the walls in the common areas and classrooms.

Are there educational posters with thinly disguised with advertising messages?

Does your school subscribe to Channel One?

If there are pop machines available to students, has the school signed an exclusive contract?

Have any curriculum materials been supplied by a company that either wants to sell a product or a point of view? (e.g., A company might supply materials for an environmental science unit that promotes their views on environmental issues.)

Are students taught how to recognize and deal with advertising on Internet sites?

Does your school teach media literacy either as a separate class or included in other classes?

If you feel advertising is a problem at your school, bring it up at a school PTA meeting. Talk to your school principal to find out what the school policies are regarding advertising in classrooms.

CHAPTER SEVEN

• • • • • • • • • •

Computers and the Internet

Scientists love to study the curve worm, with its simple brain and uncomplicated nervous system. You can literally count the neurons in its tiny body—306, to be exact. And yet, this humble, soft-bodied creature has more processing capability than a Pentium 3 computer. When you consider that human beings have one hundred billion neurons and one hundred trillion possible connections, well, it kind of puts technology into perspective. We *know* computers are just tools, but computer technology is so imbedded in everyday living that their perceived power can assume inflated proportions. Not only are personal computers fast becoming part of the landscape in our homes, but minute microprocessors are quietly thinking away in every aspect of our lives. We might not see them, but we depend on them to start the morning coffee, deliver a perfectly toasted bagel, maintain just the right climate in our automobiles.

In fact, these invisible distributed computers are as responsible for transforming our society as the multinetworked computer banks that run our workplaces. The proliferation of computer technology and, now, the Internet, have changed our culture and family life as profoundly as the arrival of television did in the fifties and sixties. In the decades since then, computer cost-effectiveness has risen one hundred-million fold: Computers today are one hundred thousand times as powerful as computers in the fifties, at one-thousandth the cost.

In doing so much for us, computers enable us to do more for ourselves. We no longer have to spend hours struggling with carbon paper and white-out; in mere seconds, we cut and paste, delete, revise, and print. Calculations that used to take tremendous amounts of effort and time are now simple and fast. We can automatically organize huge amounts of data and put it to immediate use. We can communicate ideas without regard for the constraints of distance or logistics. Through the wonders of multimedia, we can experience the sights and sounds of other places and cultures without leaving our desks. Knowledge that would have taken scientists a lifetime to develop in previous generations is ours here and now. Every accomplishment of this marvelous technology, every new capability it brings, feeds our dependency and our awe.

Yet, in our appreciation for the benefits of computers, we can overestimate their importance—and the marketers of these machines nudge us along. For its part, advertising seems to be doing a good job. Ninety percent of Americans believe that schools with computers can do a better job of educating children than schools without computers. Many believe that technology will level the playing field, and will be the answer to educating poorer children. The single most common reason parents give for purchasing a computer is that it will benefit their children's education. This last assumption might well be true, however, the mere presence of a computer is no guarantee. Although a powerful tool, there is nothing magical about a computer. How it is used and the place it is given in family life determine its potential effects.

There will be more than 500 million Internet users in the world by the year 2003.

The history of television has already taught us this lesson. The early promise that TV would raise a generation of smarter children made sense in the beginning. But, as we know, these good intentions didn't pan out. While a smattering of programming today fulfills the educational promise of television, the vast majority does not. Now, we have to manage how our children use TV and teach them to make responsible decisions. If we don't already, we'll soon find ourselves applying the same strategy to the home PC. We have to decide how it will be used, and set ground rules. We have to take a step back from marketing messages that tell us a computer will automatically make our kids smarter and give them a better education, and that a child without a computer is being robbed of opportunities to learn and grow.

Seventy percent of homes with children two to seventeen have computers. (Annenberg Public Policy Center, 2000)

A computer can certainly aid in the learning process, but it is no panacea. Nor is it necessarily an advantage. A study conducted by Professor James Kulik at the University of Michigan examined whether computer-aided instruction raised achievement scores in elementary and high schools. When computer-aided instruction was compared with the same amount of time spent learning with pencils, paper, and printed materials, the traditional way of learning proved just as effective, or better.

So, when we assume that a school with computers is automatically superior to one without them, we may be giving technology too much credit too quickly. Aside from research findings, there are other things to consider. For example, a school that invests in computer technology may do so at the expense of other programs, such as music or art. Sometimes, schools underestimate the cost of incorporating computers into a teaching environment. Purchasing and installing equipment in a school is only part of the cost; computers have to be maintained and upgraded as technology changes; teachers have to be trained. It also makes sense to wonder how a school views the role of computers in its curriculum. Are computers positioned as one learning tool among many? As the preferred resource for research and information? As a source of entertainment or reward?

For most families with a home computer, the role of their PC usually extends beyond managing family finances. The technology is a natural draw, and there are enough software options on the market to meet the interests of everyone in the family many times over. As with television, the educational value of a home computer depends on how it is used. The challenge is to decide what role it will play in your family.

If your children are babies or toddlers, the decision is a simpler one. They have only one job: to learn about their world by exploring and interacting with it. Observing, touching, tasting, listening, manipulating—this is what their play is all about. They need to experience their environment in order to wire the neurons in their brain, to establish the connections for learning and understanding they will use the rest of their lives. A desktop computer plays a limited role in this developmental process. Pressing keys and watching a screen might be interesting for a bit but, as a meaningful experience, it can't compete with pulling pots and pans out of a cupboard, feeling the cool, shiny surfaces, discovering which one fits inside which, and delighting in the clangs and bangs. There are fun and engaging software products and websites that can do a good job of introducing three-to-five-year-old children to computers and the Internet. Time should be limited for this age group, however, because learning about the world and about how to get along with others is still best accomplished through real-life experiences.

As a child enters school, a computer becomes a more useful tool. Computers provide unmatched access to information and, for children, the ability to do this is an important part of the learning process—but only a part. Children also need to develop other building blocks of academic success, including an active sense of curiosity, a lively imagination, and critical thinking skills. Some software programs can help stimulate the development of these abilities. Many, however, offer the same activities that can be done with a pencil and paper, except with bells, whistles, and fancy graphics. These programs might attract and hold your child's attention, but aren't necessarily effective learning tools. A college professor recently complained to me that computers and the Internet were not doing much to improve his students' thinking skills. Their papers looked good but, too often, the content was a demonstration of their ability for cutting and pasting; his students were becoming masters at the art of arranging data at the expense of developing original thought.

Anytime a computer enables a child to do something he can do with other tools it makes sense to ask, is this any better than the old way? Is the ability to create a painting on-screen with art software better than using brushes and an easel? Is counting computer-generated apples by dragging and dropping them into a computer-generated basket better than filling the kitchen fruit bowl with the real thing? If the answer is no, it doesn't mean you have to completely avoid the computerized re-creations of learning fun. But, you can and should assess every program with a critical eye. Compare what a software program offers with the kind of learning experience you want your child to have. Decide what the ground rules are for computer use in your house. Sit down with your child to see what a program really delivers. At the end of the chapter, you'll find tips for buying software as well as questions you should ask before making a purchase. You'll also find guidelines to help you define rules for computer use in your household.

The Internet

Now that personal computers have found their way into our homes, more and more families are experiencing technology's latest breakthrough: the Internet. As of the year 2000, 43 percent of American households were connected to the Internet, and the numbers are growing quickly. With the ability to tap into this vast global network, the power of the home computer has soared exponentially. The potential of the Internet is thrilling and, used correctly, it's an amazing resource for children and families.

The Internet is used primarily two ways: as a tool for communication and as a resource for information. Via *electronic mail* (e-mail) we are able to communicate instantly with family members and friends, wherever they are. It also lets us make new acquaintances, and learn from our information exchange. As an information resource, the Internet is infinitely large, supremely fast, and inherently efficient. In a matter of clicks, we can immediately access libraries and information the world over. The Internet is an endless, up-to-date encyclopedia complete with audio, video, graphics, and interactive capabilities.

Fifty-two percent of homes with children two to seventeen have access to the Internet. (*Annenberg Public Policy Center,* 2000.)

Along with this unprecedented level of communication and unparalleled access to information, this new technology also harbors a darker side. Like any new medium, the Internet brings new challenges and a new degree of responsibility for its users, particularly for parents and children.

The world of the Internet has evolved into three domains: information, entertainment, and commerce. The information realm hosts access to a wealth of cyberriches like libraries, art galleries, scientific sites, medical data, world cultures, and global events. With the treasure comes the trash. Because the Internet is unregulated, anyone can put any kind of information up on the net for all to see. It doesn't have to be well-researched. It can be biased, misleading, and completely inaccurate. This presents a challenge for any user but, for parents, the responsibility doubles. You not only have to teach your kids to be critical users of Internet information, but learn

Computer Myths and Facts

Myth: A computer is automatically better for children than television.

Fact: Both are powerful tools and their value depends on how each is used.

Myth: A child who is not computer literate will be unable to function in society.

Fact: In less than one month, high-school graduates who enter college with no computer experience can reach the same level of computer skills as their peers who had computers in school.

Myth: Children whose education incorporates computers do better in academic achievement tests.

Fact: Not true. Computers do not make kids smarter. There is no research to demonstrate this.

Myth: Computers are a waste of money.

Fact: Computers, like any powerful tool, are valuable if used properly.

Myth: You have to get a new computer every two years.

Fact: The speed and capacity of computers double every eighteen months, but the latest machines have powerful additions that most kids will never use or ever need.

Myth: A good parent will make sure her child has a computer.

Fact: A parent's time and attention is much more valuable than any machine.

Myth: Anyone who questions the use of computers opposes progress.

Fact: Critical questioning of anything can help us make better choices.

yourself how to determine which information is reliable. You have to develop the ability to double-check cyberfare and pass this wisdom on to your kids.

Despite the staggering power of its information-sourcing capabilities, the Internet is growing by leaps and bounds for two other reasons: its ability to entertain and its potential to facilitate commercial transactions. Just about every kid who surfs the net has played games and visited entertainment sites. Of course, there's nothing wrong with having fun—the Internet can certainly dish it out—but there's a difference between spending hours on the net researching a report and spending hours playing around. As we have throughout this book, we come back to the mantra of creating balance in the media diets of our children. Because of its boundless nature, the Internet may bring us to task on this point like no other medium. In the next few pages, we'll look at some of the less innocent fare kids can access in their quest for fun on the Internet.

Increasingly, entertainment and commerce are joining forces in cyberspace. Just as television's educational potential gave way to its value as an advertising medium, and its ability to entertain was used to deliver eyeballs to advertisers, the same pattern is emerging on the Internet. Hopefully, however, the ending will be different this time and commercial objectives won't crowd out the Internet's informational resources. Commercial use of the Internet is still in its infancy, so it's hard to know what shape its future will take. Despite all the hype about commercial potential, very few companies are turning profits via this new technology. Investment in Internet commerce today is much like railroad speculation was in the 1800s: People invested in towns in the hope and belief that the railroad would indeed go

> Teens are surfing the Internet, on average, 5.1 hours per week. (*Horizon Media Research,* 1999.)

through. While some Internet businesses will be profitable, others will not. Time will tell which models will work for which products.

While the future of business on the net remains to be seen, it's not too early for parents to be aware of what some commercial sites are doing to get ahead. Some have set their sights on, and designed their sites for, kids, using clever and often entertaining ways to extract information for marketing purposes. Recently, one site lured kids with the promise of exciting games. To access the games, kids had to join the club which, in turn, required divulging personal information about themselves, their siblings, and families. Of course, in the name of fun a child doesn't realize his privacy is being invaded.

• • • • • • • •

Children five to eighteen will spend an estimated $1.3 billion online by 2002. (*U.S. World and News Report,* November 18, 1999.)

• • • • • • • •

Other sites use microtargeting strategies to get to know their visitors: They collect very specific information and then use it to tailor commercial messages to specific individuals. For example, a site may engage a child in conversation by asking for her favorite color or favorite music. The child's answers become part of a database; the next time she visits that site the screen appears in her favorite color and the background music promotes releases from her favorite group.

The Federal Trade Commission has become involved in efforts to prohibit this kind of exploitation. In April 2000, the Child On-Line Privacy Protection Act went into effect. It is now illegal for marketers and website operators to collect personal information from children younger than thirteen without parental permission. Parents will need to remain vigilant, however: Joseph Turow of the Annenberg Public Policy Center released research in May 2000 revealing that teens are much more likely to divulge confidential family information than the younger set. Of course, the new C.O.P.P.A. law only applies to children younger than thirteen.

The Center for Media Education, in Washington, D.C., has recommended five principles that would protect children from the efforts of commercial sites:

1. Personal information should not be collected from children.
2. Advertising and promotions targeted at children should be clearly labeled as such.
3. Children's content areas should not be directly linked to advertising sites.
4. There should be no direct interaction between children and product spokescharacters.
5. There should be no online microtargeting and no direct-response marketing of children.

Until regulations are established and enforced, however, parents have to protect their children's rights and teach them to protect themselves.

Pornography on the Internet is another case in point. In 1998, buying and selling pornographic material was at the top of the list of commercial transactions on the net. The number of sites offering pornographic content is overwhelming, and many are easily accessible to children. Some sites are not only sexually explicit, but also laced with violence. Obviously, an encounter with this kind of material can be very traumatic for younger children. Older kids, naturally curious about adult sexuality, may be attracted and fascinated by these sites.

Accessing pornography on the Internet often isn't intentional. In fact, many sites count on inadvertent access. Many lure visitors with unsolicited e-mails: All you have to do is click on a link you've received and you're automatically linked to a pornography site. Others capitalize on

Fourteen percent of teen Internet users have visited sites they don't want their parents to know about. (*Pediatrics,* January 1999.)

commonly misspelled words. A simple typo can land a surfer, including a child, in the thick of pornographic content. In our own research at the National Institute on Media and the Family, we discovered that some pornography sites get you to visit and then make it difficult to leave. The Back or Exit buttons only take you deeper into the site. Before you know it, you're mired.

To help keep objectionable material at bay, you can buy filtering software that blocks your kids from accessing certain Internet sites. Be aware that no filtering software is 100 percent effective. You can be sure that pornographers, and anyone else who wants to get noticed, are always looking for ways to circumvent barriers. Ground rules for Internet use are still an essential part of the safety equation. Some families even work the placement of their home computer into the strategy. Positioning it in a high-traffic area of the house is a natural deterrent to inappropriate surfing, and lets parents monitor the activity, as well as the time spent at the computer.

Another potential danger lurking in the darkness of the Internet is the *chat rooms*. In these online meeting spaces, people can engage in conversation and form relationships with others they've never met. For an adult, the idea of talking with an invisible stranger may seem unappealing at worst (and, at best, informative and enjoyable). The image of your child doing the same thing can be absolutely frightening. The good news is that some chat rooms are well-monitored and appropriate for kids. The bad news is that some aren't. Although uncommon, there have been cases of pedophiles and sexual predators establishing relationships with kids they find in unmonitored chat rooms. Your best defense is to be clear with your kids about the rules for chat-room use. The last activity in this chapter is the construction of an Internet Safety Plan.

Only 32 percent of parents use Internet filters. (*Annenberg Public Policy Center*, 1999.)

You may want to clip it and display it next to the computer as a reminder.

Because the Internet is a mixed bag, and a vast one at that, your kids really need your guidance, whether they think so or not. As one mother said to me, "You wouldn't let your child play in the street, or get in a car with a stranger. So, I guess you can't turn him loose on the Internet either." Because the Internet is one more course in their media diet, there's no getting around being involved. Even if you aren't net worthy yet, resist the temptation to run in the other direction. The technology isn't going away, and banning the Internet from your home may mean missing out on the truly wonderful learning opportunities it has to offer.

Look at the Internet as a way to connect—not just with the wealth of cyberspace, but with your family. Surfing together promotes the Internet as a family affair, and also lets you monitor how the technology is used. By the same token, computer use in general can become something your family does as a unit, rather than time spent alone. In a very real sense, this is about creating balance. For all the good computers do, they are only one aspect among many that influence and enrich our lives. They are only one kind of connection. For our children, especially, there are so many other connections to be made, so many adventures to experience, and mysteries to explore. Computers are forever, but childhood is right now.

A Cyberhood You Can Feel Good About

Using the Internet expands your cyberhood to the far corners of the world. Children can access information and experiences from sources around the globe. Just as computers and the Internet are rich in resources, they also present special concerns for parents. How do I find safe sites for my children? What are the safety rules for children on the Internet? This chapter's activities lead you to the answers to these questions and many others.

The goal is to create a set of Household Rules for the Internet for your family. After taking a look at some Myths and Facts you'll encounter the first activity, by which you will begin to become familiar with all the typical neighborhoods on the Internet. Then, you will answer the question, "Which neighborhoods have opportunities for children and which pose some danger?"

The next activity helps you check out individual sites to see if they are appropriate for your child. Since advertising and marketing to children is a growing concern on the web, there is an activity to help you judge whether a site's activities are advertisements in disguise. Children are increasingly using the web for homework and research. Sample our favorite homework sites and use the checklists to decide if the information you're finding is reliable.

Every child using the Internet should take the Cyber Safety Quiz. Make sure that your child knows how to navigate safely on the web. Once you've finished the quiz, you will be ready to create your set of Household Rules for the Internet.

CHAPTER SEVEN ACTIVITIES

Activity: Exploring the Internet

For parents.

Whether you are currently online or not, odds are you realize that when you go out on the Internet, you have a world of resources at your fingertips.

Just as you need to be familiar with your neighborhood before you can set safety rules for your children, you also need to look around the Internet, figure out how it works, and be familiar with the safe and unsafe places for your child to visit.

Once you are familiar with the Internet, look at the Internet through your children's eyes. If your children are already Internet users, ask them to give you a tour of their favorite destinations on the Internet.

After you access the Internet, visit a variety of sites and become familiar with each of these areas:

1. *Chat Rooms.* User logs on, enters a virtual reality room and joins an ongoing, real-time discussion with messages typed in via keyboard. Learn the rules of the chat room before joining in the discussion. There are hundreds of chat rooms, some organized around interests, some designed just for kids. Some are monitored, some are not. One of the oldest chat rooms, linking children from around the world is KIDLINK, http://www.kidlink.org/rti/irc. A chat directory (not necessarily recommended for children) can be found at http://

www.liszt.com/chat. If you'd like to check out another general chat room, go to the Yahoo! site, click on "chat," and follow the directions.

2. *Newsgroups.* You will find posted messages organized around a specific topic or interest. Although there are thousands of newsgroups available, check as to which newsgroups are carried by your Internet service provider. Newsgroup readers are built into web explorers Netscape Navigator and Microsoft Internet Explorer. Once you locate a newsgroup you are interested in, you can regularly open that file, check the new information that has been posted by other members of the group, ask questions, or post your own thoughts. Remember, even in newsgroups designed for kids, adults pretending to be kids can post messages. This site lists available general newsgroups (not necessarily for children): http://www.liszt.com/news/.

3. *E-mail.* E-mail is an electronic message sent to another person or organization over the Internet. Your e-mail address identifies a site at which messages sent to you are stored until you access them.

4. *WWW site.* WWW stands for World Wide Web, and is composed of millions of sites or pages that can be reached with a click of your mouse. Each web page has a unique address, a URL (Uniform Resource Locator) that begins with http:. Visit the web page of the National Institute on Media and the Family: http://www. mediafamily.org.

5. *Mailing lists.* Also known as a *listserv,* a mailing list is similar to a newsgroup. However, you must sign up to be on a mailing list, as the postings are sent to everyone on the list via e-mail. Information on general

mailing lists and a list of the most active ones are found at http://www.liszt.com.

6. *Search engine.* This is a computer program that searches and catalogs the contents of millions of sites on the World Wide Web. A user can type search words, and the search engine will list sites matching the words. It will also provide links directly to the sites. There are many search engines. Some of the most popular are Yahoo! Alta Vista, Excite, Hotbot, and Lycos. The user accesses these search engines through their web explorer.

7. *Internet parent help site.* http://www.getnetwise. org. GetNetWise is a public-service site supported by a number of Internet corporations and public-service groups, including child-advocacy groups. This site provides an online Internet safety resource for parents and caregivers. It includes information on Internet filters, great kids' sites, kids' search engines, online safety tips, directions for reporting online trouble, and much more. Make this site your starting point in finding recommended Internet sites for children to visit.

Activity: The Internet: Treasures and Trash

For parents.

As you become familiar with the Internet, you will discover how vast it is. Because it is so enormous, there is both treasure and trash.

In the first column, rank from one to four the four areas that you are most concerned about with regard to your child on the Internet, number one being most concerned, number four, least concerned.

In the second column, identify a site where your child can safely explore exciting resources.

Column 1 **Column 2**

Chat Rooms _____   _____

Search Engines _____   _____

Newsgroups _____   _____

Web sites _____   _____

_____

_____

Activity: World Wide Web Site Checklist

For parents or parents with children ages eight and up.

Every day, thousands of sites are added to the World Wide Web. Many of these sites are aimed at children. In the past, the majority of websites for children were constructed for educational purposes by nonprofit organizations or by individuals. In the future, however, there will be more and more sites sponsored by commercial enterprises. So, how do you, as a parent, decide which sites are appropriate? Part of the answer depends on the age of your child and his or her reason for using the net. Many children access the Internet for school-related activities. Many others surf for entertainment and chat rooms.

- One tool to use is an Internet filter program. (Get-NetWise at http://www.getnetwise.org is an online Internet safety information site for parents and care-givers. As a public service, this site provides information about Internet filtering tools, kid-friendly sites, safety tips, kid search engines, and so on.)
- Another is to only use sites recommended by an au-thority you trust. For example, the American Library Association has a page for parents that lists over seven hundred sites for children at http://www.ala. org/parentspage/greatsites/amazing.html.
- Some parents build a custom web page for their child, listing the links to other web pages of which they approve.
- Other parents build an approved bookmark list for their child.

Use the following questions to help you decide if a site is one that you feel will be appropriate for your child.

1. Who created the web page?
   Has it been recommended by a child authority you are familiar with?

2. Is the web page:
   - educational in focus?
   - commercial?
   - commercial with educational activities?

3. Are the activities or the information appropriate for the age of your child?

4. Is a chat room included on the site?
If so, does it have restricted access?

5. Does the site try to gather personal information from your child (age, name, address, phone number, e-mail address, credit-card number, likes, dislikes)? Even with parental permission?

6. Does your child have to join a club in order to access part of the site?

7. If it is a commercial site are the activities used as a sales gimmick to promote certain products or brand names?

8. Is the site surrounded by advertising?

9. If it is a video game, movie, or music site, can the child access violent games, movies, or sexually inappropriate images?

10. Does the site provide unrestricted links to other sites on the web?

If you find that sites:

- are commercial, i.e., the main focus of the site seems to be advertising, you may want to limit your child's time there or eliminate it altogether
- gather marketing information from your child
- do not identify who created the page
- have your child join a club where they have to provide personal information first

- use games to sell your child a product
- allow your child to download video games, movies, or music of which you may not approve
- let the child hotlink to other sites that may not be on your safety list
- have unrestricted and unmonitored access to chat rooms

then you may want to restrict your child's access to these sites or eliminate them from your bookmarked safety list.

Activity: Children and Commercial Websites

For parents or parents with children ages four through twelve.

We've talked about the explosion of advertising on the web and how marketers are targeting children as potential customers as they visit websites. These sites do not look like traditional commercials. They are designed to be special kid-friendly sites, where your child feels a world has been created just for them.

This activity will help you identify advertising gimmicks at commercial websites so you can better protect your child from being manipulated. Often, these sites advertise themselves as worry-free zones for parents or playgrounds for children.

Go to a commercial website. Choose one your child has visited or one of these popular kids' sites.

- Nickelodeon: http://www.nick.com
- Nickelodeon Jr.: http://www.nickjr.com
- Nabisco Kids: http://www.nabiscokids.com
- Lego: http://www.lego.com
- General Mills—You Rule, School: http://www.YouRuleSchool.com/
- Kidscom: kidscom.com

See if any of these online marketing techniques are being used to manipulate your child into brand loyalty, buying merchandise, or providing personal information.

1. Does the site ask your child to register before playing the games or ask for any personal information? (Personalized greetings make the child feel the site has been created just for them.)

2. Does the site place a cookie on your computer, tracking where your child goes to collect data on your child's interests? (Cookie-placement information can usually be found by clicking on the web page's privacy policy icon, or check on your web browser.)

3. Does the site entice your child to play games and activities with brand spokespeople?

4. Is advertising woven into a game or activity? (Traditional commercials do not work on the Internet. Advertising and attempts to build brand recognition and loyalty are often woven directly into activities. For instance, a trip to Adventure World is filled with products from that company. Children do not play a game and then click on a separate commercial.)

5. In a game or activity is a child easily hyperlinked into an advertising site, then back to the game?

6. Is there product placement on the site, in games or activities?

7. Can your child color or download pictures of product characters or spokespeople? Can they send e-mail postcards from the site to friends? (Any e-mails adds to the commercial site's databases. Children can then be solicited through e-mail.)

Then:

- You may want to evaluate your child's favorite sites as to their advertising content.
- Talk with your child about how advertising at websites is different than commercials on television. Television shows break away to commercials. On the web, advertising, and entertainment are woven together.
- Visit a commercial website with your child and point out the advertising gimmicks (for example, spokespeople, product placement, cookies, advertising banners, brand names, and so on).
- *Remember,* according to many experts, children under the age of seven cannot distinguish between advertising and the activities or content of a site. Use caution with young children on the Internet.

Activity: Cybersafety Quiz

For parents and children ages five and older.

Just as you teach your child safety rules to follow when they leave the house, so you must teach safety rules to your child before they journey into the Internet world. Use this Cyber Quiz as a review, and to check your child's understanding of Internet safety.

Sit down with your child, read the question and see how well he or she scores on Cybersafety! Circle your answer, then turn the page to check against the answer key. Award a star for every right answer.

1. When on the Internet, I can use my own name because no one knows who I am or where I live.
   Yes   No

2. If I get to know someone on the Internet, then it's OK to give them my name, address, phone number, email address, or where I go to school.
   Yes   No

3. A screen name is not a person's real name. I really don't know anything about the person I'm talking to online.   True   False

4. I can trust someone I've been talking to on the Internet.   True   False   Maybe

5. If I see pictures on the Internet that are mean or make me feel uncomfortable I should:
   a. Leave the site right away.
   b. Ignore the pictures.
   c. Turn off the computer.
   d. Leave the site, find and tell an adult (parents, teacher) right away.

6. It's not a good idea for me to use bad language on the Internet, even if I see other people doing it.
   True   False

7. It's okay to set up a meeting with someone from the Internet if (circle all that apply):
   a. My parents or guardians say it's okay.
   b. They've given me their phone number and address.
   c. My parent or guardian is with me.
   d. We meet at my house.
   e. We meet in a public place.

8. If someone uses bad language on the Internet, or says something that makes me feel uncomfortable I should:
   a. Respond to them.
   b. Log off and tell an adult.
   c. Just ignore it.
   d. Show my friend and talk about what to do.

9. It's okay to e-mail my picture to someone I meet on the Internet.   True   False

10. Never share your password, even with a friend.
    True   False

11. Sometimes sites ask you to fill out a questionnaire before joining a club. This is okay to do because you are not sending the information to a person.
True   False

Answers:

1. When on the Internet I can use my own name because no one knows who I am or where I live. *No.* It's always a good idea to use a screen name for safety reasons. Also, in commercial sites, companies may be gathering information.

2. If I get to know someone on the Internet, then it's okay to give them my name, address, phone number, e-mail address, or where I go to school. *No.* Never give out any personal information without talking to your parent or guardian first and getting their permission.

3. A screen name is not a person's real name. I really don't know anything about the person I'm talking to online. *True.* That's right, the person behind the name could be anyone, adult or child.

4. I can trust someone I've been talking to on the Internet. *False.* Remember, you really do not know the identity of someone you meet on the Internet, no matter how friendly they sound.

5. If I see pictures on the Internet that are mean or make me feel uncomfortable I should:

   d.) Leave the site, find and tell a trusted adult right away.

Remember, anyone can send or put information or pictures up on the Internet. If you land in a site that makes you feel uncomfortable, tell someone right away.

If someone sends you a message that makes you feel uncomfortable, tell an adult.

6. It's not a good idea to use bad language on the Internet, even if other people are doing it. *True.* You might see bad language on the Internet, but it's best not to copy it.

7. It's okay to set up a meeting with someone from the Internet if (check ones that apply):

> a. My parents or guardian say it's okay.
> c. My parent or guardian is with me.
> e. We meet in a public place.

Never, meet with someone from the Internet unless you can check these three things.

8. If someone uses bad language on the Internet, or says something that makes me feel uncomfortable I should:

> b.) Log off and tell a trusted adult.

9. It's okay to e-mail my picture to someone I meet on the Internet. *False.* Always check with your parents before starting an email relationship with someone you meet on the net. Never send a picture without checking with them first.

10. Never share your password, even with a friend. *True.* Passwords are only for you and your family to know.

11. Sometimes sites ask you to fill out a questionnaire before joining a club. This is okay to do because you are not sending the information to a person. *False.* Many commercial sites may ask you for personal information, so that they can target ads to you. Talk to your

parents and get their okay before you fill out any questionnaire.

Activity: Web for Research

For parents and children ages ten and up

Many older children are using the vast resources of the Internet to do research for school projects or to find information about interests, hobbies, etc. Anyone can post information on the web, so it is important for children (and adults) to be able to make some judgment on whether the information is coming from a reliable source.

Use these questions to help you decide whether the information found on a web page is reliable.

1. Who created the website? _____

If the website's host is a:	the web address will end in:
• commercial business	.com
• nonprofit organization or professional or trade association	.org
• government	.gov
• school/education	.edu
• military	.mil
• networking organization	.net
• site originating in another country	address will end with the initials of that country (For example: uk, United Kingdom; jp, Japan; ca, Canada

Individuals can post their own web pages. They are usually found with a .edu, .com, or .net in their address, and may end with .html.

2. Is this organization or author credible? Are they a known source of reliable information?   Yes   No

3. When was the page created or last updated? (Check the bottom of the page.)

4. If the site gives information, does it list the source of the information?   Yes   No

5. Who was the page created for?
Adults   Teens   Children

6. Is the content mainly advertising, disguised as games or information?   Yes   No

7. Is the information presented as someone's opinion or as fact?   Opinion   Fact

Here are some great web resources for homework help:

1. http://www.slc.lib.ut.us/kidhelp.htm. The Salt Lake County Library has a great site for those beginning a research project. Divided into a wide range of categories, the pages are full of links to other sites where a student can find the sought-after information.

2. http://www.bjpinchbeck.com. Part of Discovery Channel, this site is the project of thirteen-year-old B. J. Pinchbeck and his father. Titled B. J. Pinchbeck's Homework Helper, the site provides hundreds of links to other web pages on topics that are divided by categories.

3. http://www.ipl.org. Chock full of good information, the Internet Public Library is a good stop for a student willing to spend the time. This library has a lot of rooms and spots of interest to visit.

4. http://www.schoolwork.org/. This is a fantastic site for the older student (middle school and older). Divided into categories, this site provides hundreds of links to find the information you need.

5. http://www.atlapedia.com. If you are researching countries of the world and looking for a map, Atlapedia Online is the web page for you. This site will give you physical and political color maps, as well as a host of other facts about each country.

6. http://www.homeworkcentral.com. The Homework Central website provides information for students of all ages from elementary school to college. Easy to use, this site seeks out information and organizes it for easy access by the user. This is an advertising-supported site, so students should be made aware of that.

7. http//www.yahooligans.com. A part of Yahoo! Yahooligans is a search engine just for kids. In addition to special homework pages it searches a multitude of topics.

8. http://sunsite.berkeley.edu/KidsClick!/. KidsClick! provides a treasure trove of Internet website links researched by librarians.

9. Don't forget to ask your librarian for more information and resources for your research topic.

Activity: The Computer and Your Family

For parents.

Before you create a set of family rules for Internet use, you might find it helpful to think about the suggestions here. Safe surfing requires parent supervision. Rules are important, but there are also other actions you can take.

Star any suggestions that you feel will help your child safely surf the net. Review the list after a few weeks. Check off a starred suggestion if you have acted, making it a part of your plan for your child's safe surfing.

___ 1. Keep the computer in a central location. ___
  Placing your computer in the family room, dining room, or another well-used area of the house enables you to keep an eye on it.

___ 2. With younger children, monitor or filter Internet sites. ___
  Check out GetNetWise, http://www.getnet wise.org, an online Internet safety information site for parents and caregivers. As a public service, this site gives information about Internet filtering tools, kids' sites, safety tips, kids' search engines, and so on.

___ 3. Use the computer with your child. ___
     Be there when your children are surfing the Internet. Be familiar with the sites they are visiting. Encourage your children to talk to you right away about anything on the Internet that makes them uncomfortable.

___ 4. Ask your children about the people they meet on the Internet. ___
     Make sure that your children talk to you directly about anyone they have met on the Internet who wants to meet them in person or asks for any personal information (last name, address, phone number, password).

___ 5. Don't let computers substitute for parent-child time. ___
     Ask yourself if virtual experience is as valuable as the real experience. Are computer drawing programs really better then paper and crayons?

___ 6. Have frequent discussions with your child about conversations and messages they are receiving through the Internet. ___
     Encourage your children to talk to you about any messages that are mean or make them feel uncomfortable in any way. Reassure them that it is not their fault if they get a message of that kind. Urge them to confide in you, reminding them that you are on their team. Never respond to messages that are mean, suggestive, or obscene.

Activity: Internet Safety Plan

For parents and children all ages.

As with all media, set limits on Internet use. Be clear about your rules and expectations, and let your kids know that you want them to enjoy this wonderful resource. Emphasize that the guidelines you set up will enable them to enjoy the Internet safely.

Check off any rule that you feel is important to include on your Internet Safety Plan. Discuss each rule with your children. Negotiate with your teens. Explain why it is important. List the rule on the Internet Safety Plan page. Display the rules by each computer.

___ 1. People you meet on the Internet are strangers. Do not give out personal information. Check it out with a parent. Just as they should not give out their address, telephone number, name, location of their school, or any other information to a stranger, they should not give out personal information to people they meet on the Internet, especially through chat rooms, bulletin boards, and e-mail.

___ 2. Meeting friends from the Internet in person requires a parent. Establish a firm rule with your children that they may not go to meet someone they know from the Internet unless a parent or other responsible adult goes with them. Your children should talk to you about anyone who wants to meet them or asks for any personal information.

___ 3. E-mailing personal information should only be done with permission. Explain to your children that it is not safe to e-mail a picture of themselves or anything else without first checking with you. Let them know that just as it is important that you know who their friends are and what they are doing with them, it is important that they talk with you before beginning an e-mail friendship with a new person.

___ 4. Some places on the Internet are for adults only. Let your child know that if they find themselves at an adult-only site or any site that makes them feel uncomfortable, they should leave using the back button, clicking on another bookmark site, going back to their homepage site, or just logging off. Encourage them to talk to you if they find themselves at such a site. If kids are surfing the Internet, it can be easy for them to land on an adult site.

___ 5. Set time limits. It's important to set time limits for younger children (ages twelve and under), and negotiate time limits for teens. Everyone needs to have a balance of activities in their life. Some parents allow homework time on the Internet, but limit the game playing or surfing the net to an hour a day.

OUR INTERNET SAFETY PLAN

1. _____
   _____

2. _____
   _____

3. _____
   _____

4. _____
   _____

5. _____
   _____

CHAPTER EIGHT

• • • • • • • • • •

Video and Computer Games

In 1998, I had reason to appreciate video games as never before. I was on a flight from Minneapolis to Washington, D.C., just coming in for landing at Ronald Reagan Washington National Airport. Twenty-five feet from the tarmac, our destination suddenly seemed uncertain: Another plane had pulled onto the runway in front of us. Our pilot gunned the engines and, in seconds, we were nose-up, zooming skyward. As the pilot offered reassurance over the intercom, all I could think was, thank goodness for electronic-game technology—the same basic technology used in flight simulators. A *flight simulator* is really a very elaborate video game that lets pilots practice maneuvers like the one we experienced, without risking lives. In fact, this remarkable technology is used to train all sorts of professionals, including police officers, soldiers, and medical personnel. Imagine the benefits of enabling a medical student to try out a procedure via virtual reality instead of on an actual patient.

Of course, in the beginning, video-game technology wasn't nearly so powerful. The first video game, Pong, was nothing more than a little white ball bouncing from side to side on your TV screen. From this modest debut, the technology took off like a rocket, catapulting the video and computer game business into a worldwide, multibillion-dollar industry. Sales of video and computer games have grown faster than for any other form of media. In one year alone, 1996–97, the estimated sale of electronic games increased by 50 percent.

In the course of its rapid evolution, the technology has crossed over into several forms: video, computer, handheld, and arcade games, and, most recently, online games (see chapter 7). These terms are often used interchangeably, especially by kids, and especially in reference to video and computer games. If you're just coming into it all, this can be confusing. Basically, video games are played on a TV screen via a console and cartridges you buy or rent—much like a VCR with interactive controls. Sega Dreamcast, Nintendo 64, and Sony PlayStation II are the leading video-game series you're likely to hear about from kids. Computer games are played on a PC screen via CD-ROM. The distinction seems clear enough, until you realize that most video games are now also available on CD-ROM. When in doubt, you can safely refer to any of these as *electronic games.*

• • • • • • • •
The first video game was Pong, in 1972.
• • • • • • • •

While the changes may be stunning to those of us over thirty, our kids probably can't imagine a world without video games. Twenty years ago, millions of kids were playing Pacman, that cute little dot with a mouth that munched its way across a screen; now, this game wouldn't get a second glance. In little more than two decades, game technology has gone from ping-pong to virtual reality in which the player is a character in the action—and the technology continues to advance at an amazing rate. By the end of the nineties, game technology went from 16-bit to 64-bit to 128-bit in a period of less than twenty-four months—for the speed of rendering images onscreen, the difference is analagous to a drink at the kitchen tap and a drink from a fire hydrant. The result is that game imagery is becoming more and more lifelike, and, in turn, increasingly engaging and entertaining. Realism is the ultimate goal of game technology and, of course, the ticket to bigger sales. Some industry leaders predict that within a few years games will really deliver virtual reality—the stuff of Hollywood movies right in our own hands.

Kids will be ready for it. They know all about playing electronic games. They know how to use the technology. They know what it can do, and they can make the leap to new capabilities without even thinking about it but for most moms and dads, it's a very different story. When it comes to electronic games, the knowledge gap between kids and parents is huge. The simple fact is, kids have grown up with the technology, most parents haven't. So, kids have developed the skills needed to play the games. Few adults are familiar with the technology, let alone adept at using it.

Despite the ever-widening knowledge gap, video and computer games are becoming a fixture in many families. Recent research showed that 69 percent of American families either own or rent electronic games (National Institute on Media and the Family, 1998). The same study also found that electronic games are most popular with younger kids, with the highest percentage of purchases and rentals among eight- to twelve-year-olds. In addition, kids who play electronic games do so seven hours per week on average—by comparison, the equivalent of more than a full day of school per week. Electronic games are a staple of the majority of kids' media diets, and parents have another reason to educate themselves.

Video game industry sales exceeded $20 billion worldwide in 1999.

While you may not be able to handle a joystick, you may be relieved to know that the majority of computer and video games on the market are appropriate for kids—probably 80 percent are just fine. Some games, like Myst and Riven are exceptional—these two feature spectacular graphics and marvelous stories. Others, like the Sim series and Carmen San Diego series are both educational and engaging. Playing electronic games does have some benefits. Besides being fun, it introduces kids to technology, gives them practice in problem solving and logic, helps them develop fine-motor and spatial skills, and provides an opportunity for adults and kids to play together.

However (you knew this was coming), the word on electronic games isn't *all* good. The concern is a core group of games that feature ultraviolent action. In addition to antisocial themes, they often include sex and crude language. Many parents aren't aware that these games pose a threat, in part, because they've never played them. But because they're called games, we tend to think they're harmless forms of entertainment. In fact, this segment of ultraviolents should really be renamed *kill-for-fun murder simulations*. One of the most popular games, Duke Nukem, is a case in point. In one level of Duke Nukem 3D, the player assumes the role of the title character and advances not only by killing, but by committing ever more heinous acts of violence. In one level of the game, you enter a strip joint and entice a stripper to remove her clothes. Then, you kill her, with a large helping of crude language, and sadomasochistic sex.

A field study of over five hundred parents found that 95 percent had never even heard of Duke Nukem (National Institute on Media and the Family, 1998). Yet a survey of junior high school students revealed that more than 80 percent were familiar with the game, and many had played it. Research also shows that this kind of game is particularly attractive to boys: A survey of 900 fourth through eight graders found that 50 percent favored games with violent themes (Buchman and Funk, 1996). Still other research has found that of the games most popular among kids, 80 percent feature violence (Dietz, 1998). That the vast majority of parents are unaware of games like Duke Nukem is reason enough to close the knowledge gap. However, when you consider that kill-for-fun murder simulations are games most kids are familiar with and many want to play, we can't act fast enough.

This very sentiment motivated Senators Joe Lieberman (D-Connecticut) and Herb Kohl (D-Wisconsin) to hold hearings in 1993 on the issue of violence in electronic games. As a result, the industry established a voluntary ratings system in 1994. As of this writing, virtually all the electronic games on the market today carry this ratings system. Unlike the television industry, the electronic-game industry has provided fairly accurate ratings of its fare. Games are rated on the basis of age appropriateness. The problem is that the ratings system is as foreign to most parents as the technology itself. Public education has been a weak link, and parents aren't the only ones in the dark. Forty-three percent of the store employees who sell or rent electronic games don't understand the ratings (National Institute on Media and the Family, 1998). Moreover, few retailers or rental stores have policies prohibiting the sale or rental of games rated inappropriate for kids to kids. Now consider how easy game cartridges are to pass around. Kids do it all the time.

• • • • • • • •

Eighty-two percent of youths ten to seventeen play video and computer games at home. (NPR/Kaiser/Kennedy Technology Study, 2000.)

• • • • • • • •

While there has been extensive research on the effects of TV violence, only a few studies have been conducted to date on the impact of electronic games. That's in part because the games we should be most concerned about—the ultraviolents—are fairly new to the market. As you would expect from a science-driven culture, there are those who argue that since it hasn't been proven that these games are harmful to children, we shouldn't be concerned. There are also some who propose that electronic-game violence may actually be beneficial to children because it gives them an outlet for aggression. This very same catharsis hypothesis was first advanced in the early days of the TV-violence debate. Of course, it was proved wrong. Time will tell again, I'm sure, what gut instinct (to say nothing of logic) supposes already.

For the record, the research that is appearing regarding the effects of electronic-game violence echoes the findings on TV violence. Studies show that after young children play violent video games, their behavior tends to be more aggressive. In a study of sixty boys, ages seven and eight, those who played aggressive video games exhibited more aggression in free play afterwards (Irwin and Gross, 1995). Even more recently, another study found that kids who played violent video games assigned more hostile motives to others than kids who did not play those games (Kirsch,1998). Even more convincing is a pair of studies done by Craig Anderson and Karen Dill. They found that college students who played violent video games behaved more aggressively in real life. They also discovered that violent video-game play correlated with delinquency. (Anderson and Dill, 2000) None of this should be surprising. Research aside, one thing we don't have to prove is that when a child is playing a video game, he or she is not in the role of observer, but in the role of participant. From a psychological perspective, these games are behavior rehearsals. If we use this kind of technology to train pilots, police officers, and soldiers, how could they fail to have an effect on our children? Moreover, the electronic game medium itself raises socialization issues similar to those associated with television. Since most kids not only play electronic games alone, but prefer to play alone, too much time spent playing can foster social isolation. And, when those games feature antisocial themes, the risk is compounded.

• • • • • • • • • • •

Video Game Myths and Facts

Myth: Video games have no educational value.
Fact: Many video games are educational in nature and introduce children to new technologies.

Myth: It's always easy to spot violent content in the opening levels of a game.
Fact: In some games, the violence increases as you progress through the levels.

Myth: The violence in video games does not affect the player because it is just a game.
Fact: The violence in video games may be more powerful to the player because they are actively participating, instead of passively watching.

Myth: Children understand the difference between the real world and fantasy.
Fact: For the younger child, especially, the line between reality and fantasy is less than crystal clear. Some react to fantasy violence as if it were real.

Myth: Playing video games is a good alternative to watching television.
Fact: Parents should monitor video-game playing the same way that they monitor television viewing.

Myth: Stores that sell or rent video games will not sell or rent mature or adult games to children.
Fact: Very few stores have policies or enforce policies that prevent children from buying or renting games that are rated for an adult customer.

Myth: Violence and profanity are present only in games that are rated for mature users.

• • • • • • • • • • •

● ● ● ● ● ● ● ● ● ● ●

Fact: Minimal violence and crude language may be present in a
        game rated acceptable for children as young as six years
        of age.

Myth: Playing video games always isolates the child because he or
        she always plays alone.

Fact: Buying games that require two or more players will encour-
        age socializing. Also playing games with your child will en-
        courage family interaction.

● ● ● ● ● ● ● ● ● ● ●

Perhaps the most significant report to date on the implications of electronic-game violence comes from Lieutenant
Colonel David Grossman, author of the book *On Killing*. Before retiring from the military, Grossman spent more than
twenty-five years studying how to enable soldiers to kill.
Today, he is an acknowledged expert on killology. Because
killing does not come naturally, the armed forces have developed specific programs that train soldiers to kill. The biggest
barrier to killing is the psychological resistance, not the technical skills involved in firing a weapon. In his book, Grossman
explains how psychological conditioning techniques were sys-
tematically applied to successfully eliminate that resistance.
In recent writings and interviews he has been very clear: The
techniques used by the army to enable soldiers to kill are the
very same techniques used in today's violent electronic games.
"Children don't naturally kill; they learn it from violence in
the home, and most pervasively from violence as entertainment in television, movies and interactive video games."
(Grossman, 1998).

Despite such insight, producers of ultraviolent games are
likely to keep pushing the envelope to see how far they can go.
As we know from television's example, the pursuit of profit

rules. In fact, the marketing of these games says as much. Even though ultraviolent games are rated inappropriate for children, there is evidence that some of the ultraviolent games are being marketed to kids. *Sports Illustrated for Kids* featured an advertisement for the ultraviolent video game Resident Evil II. A walk down a toy-store aisle will turn up Duke Nukem and Resident Evil II action figures for sale.

In addition, the advertising messages themselves are disturbing—even for games rated suitable for kids. For example, the ad slogan for Point Blank, rated T, for teenagers, promises: "More fun than shooting your neighbor's cat." An ad for Subspace, a game rated KA (kid-to-adult), declares: "Meet people from all over the world, then kill them." Even game hardware doesn't escape unconscionable marketing ploys. An ad for a new joystick system boasts: "Great! You get better accuracy and control, but what are you going to do with all the extra bodies? Be the first on your block to make your neighbors say, what's that smell?" It doesn't take much analysis to conclude that marketing techniques like these are sending the wrong messages to kids.

Since there are good games on the market for kids, and because kids are so familiar with the ultraviolent games, parents need to become better informed about the options, and more involved in their child's game use. One of the most valuable tools available to parents is the Video and Computer Game Report Card. Produced annually by the National Institute on Media and the Family, the Report Card offers a snapshot view of industry trends and ratings policies, as well as parent-generated evaluations of some of the most popular games. The Report Card has brought about several important changes in the electronic game industry: ratings for all games, an advertising code of conduct, and the industry's agreement to educate the public about the ratings. Like the KidScore ratings system for television programming, the Video and Computer Game Report Card puts power into the hands of parents by helping them build their media knowledge base. The more you know about electronic games, the better, more informed decisions you can make for you children. You can access the Report Card via website: http://www.mediafamily.org, or receive a copy of the report by contacting the National Institute on Media and the Family (address and phone number on back cover of this book).

The Cyberhood Map

Video games have become an important part of our children's media lives. As with other forms of media, there are games that are great for kids, and others that have no place in our homes. We need to monitor video and computer games the same way in which we monitor television and movies

The goal of this chapter's activities is to create a set of Family Video Game Rules. Before doing that, however, there are activities that will help familiarize you with the range of games, and the ratings. Tips for choosing games then leads to the last activity, creating your family rules.

• • • • • • • • • • • •

CHAPTER EIGHT ACTIVITIES

Activity: Visit a Video-Game Arcade

For parents.

Video-game arcades are popular places for game players. Companies often test new games in the arcade market. Home versions of these games often then end up on store shelves. Unfortunately, some of the most popular games at arcades are the games with the most violence. Often, there is little or no attempt by the managers of arcades to prevent younger children from playing adult or mature games. A visit to an arcade can benefit the parent in two ways: First, a parent can check out the games and see if ratings are posted or enforced; second, a parent can watch popular games being played and check out the content of more advanced levels.

Visit a video game arcade in your neighborhood or at the local mall. Answer these questions and see what games are most popular.

1. Are ratings posted on each game? Yes No (The arcade industry uses a green, yellow, red sticker system for each game.)

2. What games are most kids playing? _____ _____

3. How many games have violent content? _____ _____

• • • • • • • • • • • •

4. How are women portrayed in the games? _____
_____

5. What kind of supervision is there? _____
_____

6. Are younger kids restricted from playing games rated for older players?   Yes   No

Activity: Video Game Ratings

For parents.

It's often difficult for parents to know whether a game is appropriate for their children because they do not play the more advanced levels. The industry's video-game ratings are, therefore, a big help. Almost all games are now rated and the ratings are printed on the box. Created by the Entertainment Software Rating Board (ESRB), the ratings on page 192 describe video-game content based only on age-appropriateness. For a full list of detailed content descriptors (i.e., mild animated violence, suggestive themes, etc.), you can visit the ESRB web site at www.esrb.org.

Look over the video games in your own home collection. Find the game ratings.

How many games do you own in each category? Are the games your children play appropriate for their age level?

Video-game ratings carry one of six logos, showing age recommendations:

 Early Childhood: Content suitable for children ages three and older.

 Everyone: Content suitable for persons ages six and older.

 Teen: Content suitable for persons ages thirteen and older.

 Mature: Content suitable for ages seventeen and older.

 Adults Only: Contents suitable only for adults.

 Rating Pending: Product has been submitted to the ESRB and is awaiting final rating.

Other resources for information include nonindustry ratings, such as our KidScore rating from the National Institute on Media and the Family.

Activity: Checking a Game Before You Buy

For parents.

Now that you have checked out your family collection of video games, how about new games? Hundreds of new video games come on the market each year. How do you evaluate a game to see if it is appropriate for your child? This checklist will give you some ideas.

Use the questions below to help you evaluate a video game before you buy it for your child.

1. Was the game recommended to you by a source you trust?   Yes   No

2. Has the game been evaluated by a nonindustry source, so you can get some idea as to content? Yes   No

3. Is the industry game rating on the box? Yes   No

4. Does the age rating match the age of your child? Yes   No

5. Does this game fall into the educational category? Yes   No
   Or is it entertainment?   Yes   No

6. Is the game primarily a shoot, punch, or kick game?   Yes   No

7. Are there women or girl characters in this game? Yes   No

8. If so, how are they portrayed? _____

9. Does the violence in the game become more intense as the player advances through levels? Yes   No

10. Does this game require that the player use any higher order thinking skills in planning, organizing, or evaluating the game situations? Yes   No

11. Does this game help your child acquire a skill? Yes   No

As you can see when considering the value of a game for your child, there are many things to consider. Here are some tips to help you:

- Be aware of how games are marketed to children.
- Look at the game ratings to help you make a judgment about the content.
- Check out nonindustry ratings and recommendations.
- Pick games for a young child, and make sure an older child gets your approval when he or she is choosing a game.
- If possible, rent a game to preview it before buying it.
- If there are violent or sexual themes in the title or cover picture, you can assume that these themes are in the game.

- Look for games involving two people to encourage group play.
- Select games that are mentally stimulating, not just shoot and punch.
- Look for a game that requires the player to come up with strategies and solve problems. Point-and-shoot games don't usually require much brain power.

Activity: Ideas to Think About

For parents.

Before sitting down with your family to discuss rules for video game use, it is often helpful to consider some ideas first. When you do, you're on the road to healthy media use!

Read each suggestion. Check the ones you think are important to include in your family plan. Are there any you might start right away?

_____ 1. Limit game-playing time. (I would recommend no more than one hour per day.)

_____ 2. Check the ratings on the box to see if it is age appropriate.

_____ 3. For any games with violent or sexually suggestive themes, preview to determine whether you feel content is appropriate for your child.

_____ 4. Play with your child to become familiar with the games.

____ 5. Require that homework and jobs be done first; use video-game playing as a reward.

____ 6. Do not put a video game set in children's rooms where they can shut the door and isolate themselves.

____ 7. Talk with your child about the content of the games.

____ 8. Ask your video store to require parental approval for kids to rent a violently rated video game.

Activity: Family Plan for Video-Game Use

For parents or parents and children ages four and up.

The use of video games as entertainment for children has exploded within the last decade. Most children either have video or computer games in their homes, play at friends' homes, or play in video arcades. Even though there are many fun, worthwhile games on the market, many game makers use violence, profanity, and sex to sell their games. Because of this, and because of the tendency of young players to spend a significant amount of time playing, parents need to monitor their child's game playing the same way they monitor television viewing.

Read each question or situation. Discuss and decide if this is an area you want to include in your plan for family video-game use.

When there is disagreement, try to negotiate a compromise when appropriate. Write down your family's plan for video-game use.

1. *Time.* Some kids play alone each day. Other kids make video game playing the number-one activity they do with friends. How much time do you think your child should spend playing video or computer games each day?

_____

_____

2. *When.* Many kids will start a game before breakfast or whenever they feel bored. Some kids spend a lot of time playing video games rather than doing homework. When do you feel you want your child to be able to play his/her video games?

_____

_____

3. *Game ratings.* Every game on the market now has a game rating. Unfortunately, some of the most popular games on the market contain violence, profanity, and more explicit sex than most parents want for their children. The game ratings on the box are there to help parents begin to make a judgment as to the appropriateness of the content of the game for their child. What rating levels do you feel are appropriate for your child? (EC, early childhood; E, everyone; T, teens; M, mature; AO, adult only)?

_____

_____

4. *Parent approval.* Game ratings only begin to help a parent make a decision as to whether a game is appropriate. It's important for a parent to have some sense of what the content of a game is, to see the game up on the screen, or read reviews of the game from a source you trust. Do you want to have parental approval over games your child plays, whether they are rented, bought, or received as gifts? _____

5. *Number of games.* Some parents have found it helpful to limit the number of video or computer games they buy their children. Limiting the number of video games helps in several ways: First, it gives the parent time to make an informed choice of a fun, interactive, appropriate game. Two, besides saving money, it cuts out pressured, impulse buying. Three, it helps the child think about what they might really enjoy playing, and leaves room in their life for other kinds of activities. Do you feel that limiting the number of video or computer games you buy would be helpful in monitoring game use? _____

If so, how many games do you feel you would buy for your child per year and for what occasions?

_____

_____

6. *What to do when friends come over.* Some parents worry when their child's friends come over, and the first and main choice of play is video games. Encouraging alternate activities is important, especially when they can get outside and play. Some parents solve this dilemma by putting a time limit on video play (also making it a

part of their child's daily limit) or by making it a family rule that video-game playing cannot be the first choice. Do you want to make a family rule about group video-game playing? _____

If so, do you feel a time limit alone would be helpful, or would you combine a time limit with other activity choices first?

_____

_____

Now, it's time to write out the plan for your family's use of video games. You may have decided that it's necessary to limit only the number of games purchased or rented, or perhaps you feel it's also necessary to limit time and kinds of games, too. What's important is that you as the parent get involved in monitoring your child's video-game use.

Make a list now of the rules you feel are important for your family's video game use, discuss them, and post them near the video-game player for referral.

FAMILY VIDEO GAME PLAN

1. *Time limit.* _____

_____

_____

2. *When.* _____

_____

_____

•   •   •   •   •   •   •   •   •   •   •

3. *Game ratings.* _____

_____

_____

4. *Parent approval.* _____

_____

_____

5. *Number of games.* _____

_____

_____

6. *Rules for play with friends.* _____

_____

_____

Getting comfortable with the world of electronic games may seem a daunting prospect to many parents, because it is such alien territory. But, as with any other form of media, there really is no other alternative if you want to have an influence on your child's media experiences and habits. And, now that you know why you should get involved, it's harder to turn a blind eye. Keep in mind, however, that you don't have to become a skilled gamer to make changes for the better. You can leave the prowess to your kids if you want to. You don't have to assume the role of Big Brother, but you do need to know what games your kids are playing, where they're playing them, and with whom. Being involved

•   •   •   •   •   •   •   •   •   •   •

may help your kids make better decisions in the face of temptation and peer pressure. At the very least, knowing that you know gives them a sense of security, even if they don't show it.

CHAPTER NINE

. . . .

Music

> De gustibus non est disputandum.
> (It is impossible to argue matters of taste.)
>
> ——Ancient Roman saying

If the Romans of Cicero's day could don headphones and
sample today's CDs, no doubt they would have included music
among "matters of taste." Especially if they had teenagers at
home. The clash between parents and kids over music has become a rite of passage. Parents of the fifties wrung their hands
in despair, sure that Elvis Presely would corrupt an entire generation of youth. A decade later, parents were up in arms about
a foursome of longhairs from Liverpool. Today, the music industry churns out artists and genres as fast as it can burn a
laser disc, giving parents and kids proportionally more opportunities to butt heads over everything from heavy metal to
gangsta rap. These artists make it their business to push limits
and rewrite moral codes. To be sure, plenty of parents still
worry about what music is doing to their kids.

However, if history is any indication, parents and teens

would be at odds over music no matter what it sounded like. Music is here to stay, adolescence is as inevitable as taxes, and the pairing can be combustible. Of course, that's not much of a consolation if you're in the thick of it. You may not be trying to change history, but you do have to muddle through this. The truth is, you don't have to feel utterly powerless. Understanding what's behind the struggle may be more enlightening than you think it is, and it will give you something to work with rather than against.

When it comes to music, parents and teens have different perspectives, motivations, needs, and expectations. Let's begin with the adult's view of the matter. Whether we realize it or not, we carry with us certain opinions and beliefs about music. What kind of music is music to your ears? Classical, country, jazz, rock, pop, instrumental, opera, or something else altogether? What isn't? Depending on your personal tastes, the same list might apply. Matters of taste notwithstanding, however, most of us agree that music is enjoyable. We're attracted to its rhythms and melodies because it makes us feel something: a surge of excitement as the school band plays the team song, a burst of pride as a skilled voice belts out the national anthem, a rush of tender feelings as a love song unfolds. And then there are the memories we associate with certain songs—who hasn't had the past come rushing back while listening to a few familiar bars? We don't need scientific research to tell us that music is enjoyable or that it affects our emotions. We know this firsthand.

However, science—and sometimes what we *think* is science—can influence what we believe about music. Take the popular notion that infants who listen to classical music will grow up to be geniuses. Many a parent has added this to their music belief system. The claim isn't actually scientific fact, though scientific research did plant the seed. Studies have shown that classical music stimulates the same part of the brain that manages spatiotemporal relations, the cognitive skills used in math, science, and engineering. So, a theory was tested: that listening to classical music would increase the ability to perform spatiotemporal tasks. The results did confirm a link. Naturally, the finding garnered a lot of press, and sent a lot of parents and prospective parents shopping for classical music. However, what didn't get reported to the masses was that the advantage was short term, lasting only ten to fifteen minutes, nor did the media coverage make clear that the research was conducted on college students, not infants or young children. In truth, there is no evidence that classical music will make a genius of your child. No matter, a theory was already on its way to becoming a widely held belief.

Another study made a related and important discovery: It found that playing, rather than listening to, music held the key to improved cognitive ability. In the study, preschool children who were given piano lessons for several months did better on spatial reasoning tasks than children who had been given computer lessons or nothing at all. They actually improved their ability to work puzzles and other tasks by as much as 30 percent. Indeed, there seems to be some lasting cognitive value in teaching children to play music, but music lessons are still no guarantee your child will turn out to be a genius.

Just as we may ascribe positive influences to certain kinds of music, we may also assume that some popular fears about music are based in reality. For example, many people are convinced that modern rock is creating a culture of delinquent youth. Parents have led crusades to ban offensive music and held bonfires to destroy these evil recordings. Even if you're a far cry from leading a movement, what you hear can play into your fears. You wouldn't be the first to wonder if offensive music was doing your children any harm. If you consider that music has the power to positively affect emotion, you might easily wonder if it can negatively affect behavior.

This very concern was expressed by columnist Al Hunt of *The Wall Street Journal* when he wrote, "If Frank Sinatra songs make people feel romantic and John Philip Sousa makes people feel patriotic, then the obscene violence of shock rocker Marilyn Manson or gangsta-rapper Snoop Doggy Dog might encourage impressionable and troubled teenagers to feel perverted or violent" (*The Wall Street Journal,* June 11, 1998). It may be somewhat reassuring to know that research has found no evidence of music having profound effects on kids in general. This doesn't mean there's no reason to object to what your child brings home, but it may take the edge off your worries. Later in the chapter, we'll look at concerns parents commonly have about music and what research has to say about these issues.

Whether it's experience, opinion, hearsay, or science, what we believe about music does shape our hopes and fears about its place in our children's lives. When your child is young, you may hope that music will be a source of joy and an opportunity to explore sounds and rhythms, so you buy music for her to listen to and instruments to play with. Everything proceeds swimmingly for awhile. You are in total control: You choose what she listens to, you make the purchases. Music is a positive experience and you have little reason for concern.

Ninety-six percent of teens listen to the radio at least once a week.

Then, she approaches adolescence, and control starts slipping through your fingers. Now, she has her own opinions about what she likes to listen to and the money to express that opinion with her purchases. When her taste collides with yours—as it commonly does between parents and budding adolescents—the conditions are ripe for conflict. Whether her musical choices are annoying, worrisome, or downright offensive, you've entered new territory. Your initial hope (that music would be enjoyable) hasn't changed, but the terms certainly have.

So, there you are with your beliefs, opinions, and expectations, and here comes your child chock full of adolescence. Not that it's news to you if you're raising a teenager, but adolescence is a time of transformation to beat all before it or to come. In no stage of your child's development has change loomed so big. I often refer to adolescence as a "normally abnormal" period of life. We all entered adolescence children and emerge adults. Physical changes are matched in force by a struggle for identity on the inside. Everything adolescents think about, feel, and do is inseparable from the struggle to become themselves. It's no wonder they experience emotions with such intensity.

Until now, you've probably controlled much of your child's life: where he lives, where he goes to school, when he goes to bed—and his values once echoed your own. In adolescence he begins asking "Who am I?" Inevitably, a part of the answer is "I am not my parents." He begins to withdraw from adults in general and puts distance between himself and you. Peers become very important, because they offer clues on how to behave and how to be accepted. Awakening sexuality and romance are thrilling and frightening at the same time. As he tries to figure out his feelings he naturally becomes self-absorbed and reflective. He dabbles with ways of presenting his emerging identity, trying them on to see what fits. He may well adopt positions contrary to yours (even enjoying it!) on everything from long hair, to piercing, to music you think is trash.

Music is a common hot button. Studies show that as kids enter the teenage years, they develop a greater interest in music than at any other age. In fact, as they move further into adolescence, they actually spend less time watching TV and more time listening to music. Music retains a position of importance for many kids for quite some time.

Considering the vortex of adolescence, we shouldn't be surprised that music is so important to teenagers. Music and adolescence were made for each other. With its power to trigger emotions, reinforce feelings, create and change moods, music speaks to the adolescent experience. It appeals to the all-consuming need to understand and be understood. Its themes and lyrics provide release, reward, clarity, and comfort. And it provides a vehicle for distinguishing identity. In the struggle to stand apart from adults—particularly parents—adolescents find music a perfect vehicle of expression. They can explore themselves by experimenting with different kinds of music and dressing or behaving in a way associated with its creators. Music becomes a way of bonding with peers and defining themselves as part of a group. And often it can be a way of shutting down communication with you.

• • • • • • • •

Forty percent of all of music purchases in the U.S. are made by people under twenty-four.

• • • • • • • •

I've heard the same story from parents countless times: headphones that become part of daily attire, closed bedroom doors and walls that vibrate, and car radios cranked to avoid conversation.

While all this behavior is normal for teenagers, it can be trying for parents and families. Concerns and questions about your child's music habits only add to the stress. In certain cases, your worries really are nothing to worry about. In others, your parental radar is on the money. Here are several issues parents frequently wonder about, along with feedback based on research results and expert opinion.

Lyrics

Many parents are concerned about the lyrics their kids are listening to, particularly lyrics that feature violence, defiance, rebellion, and sex. At best, these themes can be offensive to adult ears, and, at worst, plant seeds of worry in a parent's heart. Plenty of parents object to the sexual language in some music. There seems to be more and more of it all the time. Studies, in fact, reveal that this is true. In 1980, 4 percent of songs on the air contained explicit sexual references. By 1990 the percentage had risen nearly fourfold. Parents also often wonder if rebellious lyrics encourage their teens to act out. For these parents, it may help to remember that themes of rebellion and defiance have long found a voice in music. Social ills and controversies have given generations of musicians and songwriters cause for artistic expression. And, because adolescence itself is about rebelling, for many kids, music becomes a symbolic way of doing just that.

> On average, American teens listen to music or watch music videos between four and five hours a day.

That said, the most reassuring and important thing to consider may be this: That while parents zero in on what songs are saying to their kids, kids tend to relate to the music. For kids, lyrics actually take a back seat to the more powerful draw of the music itself: its ability to evoke feelings. The exception is rap music. In this case, lyrics are the main attraction, and parents may have more reason to take issue with the messages their kids are hearing. But whatever they're listening to we do have a right and responsibility to let our children know that certain music offends us and that we won't listen to it in our homes.

Music and Academic Performance

If your child never hits the books without turning on the music, you may worry her concentration is getting short shrift. One recent survey found that 58 percent of high school students study this way on a regular basis. The consensus is, however, that as long as your child is able to study and complete homework assignments, you probably don't need to worry. If on the other hand, there's a lot of listening going on and no homework getting done, you may have to set up some ground rules. Studies suggest that few kids spend their time just listening to music; they tend to listen to music while doing other things.

Heavy Metal Music

Understandably, parents worry about the focus of this kind of music, some of which even glorifies Satanism and the occult. Research does suggest, however, that for most kids, interest in heavy metal is a passing fad. Heavy metal tends to be most popular in early and middle adolescence and loses its attraction as kids mature. However, studies also show that some kids who become immersed in this genre can be adversely affected by it. Because these kids usually have other problems—authority issues, drug use, legal offenses, poor academic performance—it's hard to tell which comes first. The likelihood is that heavy metal music isn't a cause of problem behaviors, but rather is especially appealing to troubled kids. For them, a steady diet of heavy-metal music may be symptomatic of significant underlying issues and, therefore, a cry for help.

MTV

When MTV was born in 1981, it changed the way music was delivered. It began as a perpetual advertisement intended to provide exposure to records and CDs. It became phenomenally successful and popular among teens and young adults. The entertainment world now refers to kids eighteen and younger as *MTV babies,* because they were raised on this new breed of music advertising. MTV continues to be popular with kids, particularly teenagers. Studies show that 35 percent to 40 percent of teens watch some music videos on a daily basis. This alone

Seventy-five percent of nine to twelve-year-olds report they watch music videos at least occasionally.

should invite parents to pay attention to how their children are spending their time, but the unique power of this medium is another reason to take notice. MTV combines the emotional effects of music with the magnetic draw of visual imagery, boosting both its appeal and its power. Frequently, what it communicates is reason for concern. MTV videos often feature graphic sexual behavior, violence, and offensive portrayals of gender roles. Studies in fact show that teenagers who watch a lot of MTV have more permissive attitudes about premarital sex than kids who watch little or none at all.

Hearing Loss

This issue is getting a lot of attention from the medical community. Physicians are increasingly concerned that listening habits among teens are paving the way for hearing loss. Hearing may be affected by music played at ninety decibels. Rock concerts and music clubs typically exceed this level by quite a bit, but even school dances frequently play music at potentially damaging levels. Unfortunately, hearing loss is not easily detected because it happens gradually. By the time a problem is discovered, substantial and irreversible damage may have occurred.

Whatever issues you're coping with, the challenge is to find a balance that everyone can live with. Respect your child's need to explore his identity, but also preserve the ground rules of your household. Since adolescents commonly withdraw from parents, struggles over music can drive the wedge even deeper. This doesn't mean you have to walk on eggshells, but you can approach the issue in ways that help keep the two of you connected. Pay attention to what your child is listening to. Be genuinely interested, ask questions, and talk about music without judging. My wife came up with a great way of keeping the lines of communication open with one of our teenagers. She asked our daughter to record a mix of songs on tape for a birthday present—not songs my wife would like, but songs my daughter favored. It turned out to be a good experience for both of

Exposure to sound levels in the 90 to 140 decibel range over time will lead to hearing damage.

Music Myths and Facts

Myth: All music videos are bad for kids.
Fact: Generalizations don't work here. Some music videos are beautiful works of art; others are laced with sex and violence.

Myth: Any music recording with offensive language is clearly labeled.
Fact: The Parental Advisory sticker system is completely voluntary, not all recordings with offensive language carry the sticker.

Myth: Television composes the main part of a teenager's media diet.
Fact: Teenagers spend between four and five hours a day listening to music. Many teenagers start to substitute listening to music for TV time.

Myth: The majority of teenagers' lives are wrapped up in rebellious crisis and conflict with those around them as reflected in the news, music, and print media.
Fact: Most teenagers are not at risk, and are not in a constant state of crisis.

Myth: Music videos are just entertainment.
Fact: Many teens gather information about dress, what slang is "in," topics of conversation, and social and political ideas from music videos.

Myth: Music is just music.
Fact: There are many categories of teen music (punk, rock, rap, hip hop, alternative, folk, reggae, heavy metal, etc.) and many social groups of teens are identified by the type of music they listen to.

Myth: Teens listen only to the sound of the music, not the lyrics.
Fact: The more a teen is involved in a particular type of music, the more important the words are.

them. My wife learned about the music that was important to our daughter, and our daughter felt proud and valued.

In the process of being accepting and respectful, you can also be clear about what you will not tolerate in your home. Your gut reaction might be to forbid your teen from buying or listening to music you find offensive but, of course, this is an unrealistic expectation. What your child listens to when driving around with friends, or what CDs he chooses to spend his money on, are usually beyond your control. But you can set limits on the music that is played in family listening space. You can explain that you don't appreciate certain music and why. Stick to value-based reasons for your objections rather than labeling. For example, you might explain that you don't want to hear certain music because "it objectifies women," or ". . . talks about drug use," or ". . . expresses violence," rather than because "it's not even music . . . it's garbage . . . it's a waste of time." Let him know you realize you can't keep him from listening to such music, but that the rest of the family doesn't want to hear it.

If getting a handle on MTV becomes an issue for you, treat it as you would TV in general: Limit the amount and type of programming watched. If the rules aren't working and you find yourself in a never-ending MTV battle, remember that it's a cable subscription service; you can request a channel block anytime you like.

In one way or another, all the strategies you put to use in your struggle to end struggles over music are about preserving health: your sanity, your relationship with your teenager, your family rules and boundaries, and your child's hearing. I can almost hear the collective groan from parents who know what's coming—earplugs, oh sure. I can't get him to hang up his clothes, let alone wear earplugs. She'll never go for it, they're not cool. Unfortunately, hearing loss is a real threat for current generations of kids. Popular music culture has always had an affinity for soaring decibel levels. Big sound is part of the concert experience. Today, big sound has also become integral to other forms of entertainment media. Sound technology has brought the capabilities of Dolby and Surround Sound to our movie theaters and into our homes. Now, the ultrarealistic visual special effects we see on screen are matched in kind by hyperrealistic audio effects. And volume is part of the magic. It makes the experience more real. Pumped-up volume levels are part of the entertainment value. They've become part of our entertainment culture.

So, getting your child to take his hearing seriously may take some doing. But, while it's impossible to keep him from the fun, it is worth giving some talk time to the risk of listening to loud music. Nothing preachy, nothing technical, just the truth: Loud music damages hearing; you can't tell it's happening; by the time you can, it's too late; hearing loss is permanent. Then, give him a set of earplugs. Tell him that most rock musicians wear them. Give him several sets. Give all of his friends a set. And tell him the choice is his.

Cyberhood Map

For most preteens and teens, music is at the center of their social life. They spend more and more time listening and they can have intense loyalty to the latest singer or group. The activities in this chapter will help you open up lines of communication with your child about his or her music.

The goals of these activities are to:
- offer some suggestions about making music part of your baby's and toddler's life.
- think about guidelines, especially for your younger child (ages eight to twelve).
- communicate with your teenagers about music.

CHAPTER NINE ACTIVITIES

Activity: Listen and Remember

For parents.

Music is the media of choice for many teenagers. Think of the music you like or dislike. Why do you enjoy the music you listen to? How does it make you feel? Although you may not like certain types of music, there are many other people who do. Why?

Musical tastes are very personal. That is why talking about music with your teens can be very touchy. If you happen to dislike their choice of music and say so in a very negative way, they may take it as a personal attack. If you wish to understand your teenager better, music can be an opportunity to listen to your child talk about what's important to him or her.

Before you launch into a discussion with your teen, however, it might be a good idea for you to get in touch with some of your own memories of music listening as a teenager.

Sit, relax, and let your mind wander back to when you were a teenager and the music that was important in your life. If you've saved any of those old recordings, put the music on and think back to where and why you listened.

1. Who were three of your favorite bands or singers?

_____

2. Can you remember any of your favorite songs? (Can you remember the first song or piece of music that you really liked?)

_____

_____

3. Can you remember where you were when you usually listened to music? Were you by yourself or with friends?

_____

4. How did your favorite music make you feel?

_____

5. What was going on in the world around you as a teenager? What was the world like? How did your music respond to or mirror your world?

_____

_____

_____

6. Did you have disagreements with your parents over your choice of music? _____ If yes, how were those disagreements handled? _____

_____

Do you think they were handled well? _____

If yes, why? _____

If not, why not? _____

· · · · · · · · · · · · ·

If you've been able to get in touch with any of these feel-ings and memories, you are well on your way to being able to listen and learn about teens' music today.

Activity: Make a Tape

For parents, teens, and preteens.

Ask your son or daughter if he or she would loan you a few of their favorite CDs, or ask them to make you a tape mix of their favorite songs. If it's near a holiday or your birthday, ask them for it as a present.

Before you listen, think for a moment of what a teen's world is like today: fast paced, media saturated, adult oriented, diverse, pressure filled, sometimes lonely, peer oriented, worldwide in scope, instantaneous, and filled with work and school. Remember that music is often a reflection of the society. So, now spend some time listening. You needn't crank up the volume the way your teen does.

You may enjoy this music or you may not.

You may understand it or you may not.

What's important is to listen to the music, so you can listen to your son or daughter and why they like it.

· · · · · · · · · · · ·

Activity: Music Talk

For parents and teens.

Now that you have taken time to listen to some of your teen's music and thought about why music was important to you, you should talk to your teen.

Perhaps you enjoyed her music and just want to share that.

Perhaps you want to listen to your teen talk about what he likes most about his music.

Perhaps you found some music offensive and are concerned.

Listen to your teen's music with her. Engage your teen in a discussion of some of the same questions you asked yourself in the earlier activity.

- What's his favorite song?
- What does he like about the music you are listening to?
- What is the musician trying to say or make you feel?

If you find some of the lyrics offensive, have your child tell you why they would want to listen to it. Be clear about your own values, and what you will or will not want broadcast in the house, but let your teenager make their own decision about what they want to listen to privately.

Have clear guidelines with younger children (ages eight to twelve) concerning music with offensive lyrics.

If you've brought understanding and a listening ear to the conversation, then perhaps you've been able to open an all-important line of communication with your son or daughter on what they value, and perhaps your values as well. If a conversation was not fruitful, be patient and keep listening. Be there and eventually you'll make a connection.

Activity: Suggestions and Guidelines

For parents.

Nurture your child's musical life. Start before your child is born. Children love music. Music brings a richness that lasts a lifetime.

Check the suggestions that will help you bring music into the life of your child. Set clear family guidelines with your preteen concerning music with objectionable lyrics. Negotiate music guidelines with your teen.

For the younger child (infancy through age seven):

_____ 1. Introduce a variety of music to your child early in life.

_____ 2. Listen to music together.

_____ 3. Sing baby rhymes and nursery rhymes to your infant and toddler.

_____ 4. Bring your young child to hear live music.

_____ 5. If possible, encourage your child to play a musical instrument.

_____ 6. Make homemade hand instruments (rattles, shakers, etc.) with your child.

_____ 7. Small children cannot listen to music and not dance. Dance with your baby to music you love.

_____ 8. Sing to your infant often.

For your preteenager (ages eight to twelve):

_____ 1. Play a variety of music in your home.

_____ 2. Listen to the music your child listens to.

_____ 3. Watch the music videos your child might be watching.

_____ 4. Bring your child to hear live music.

_____ 5. Early on, establish family guidelines on music with objectionable lyrics.

For your teen:

_____ 1. Play a variety of music in your home.

_____ 2. Listen to the music your child listens to.

_____ 3. Watch the music videos your child might be watching.

_____ 4. Use music as an opportunity to talk to your child about what's important to her.

_____ 5. Be clear about your own values and family values and, thus, what can and cannot be played throughout the house.
- Include your teen in lots of discussion.
- Listen to your teen's view.
- Negotiate, do not dictate.

_____ 6. Listening is more helpful than general condemnation, if you don't like your child's music.

_____ 7. Watch out for power struggles as your child gets older. Music often needlessly becomes a battleground for parents and teens.

_____ 8. Keep lines of communication with your older child open.

CHAPTER TEN

• • • • • • • • • •

Reading and Media

> *If you want your children to be brilliant,*
> *read them fairytales. If you want them to be*
> *more brilliant, read them more fairytales.*
>
> ——Albert Einstein

Every time you read to your child, you are helping her de-velop the capacity to understand and use language. At the same time, her growing facility with language stimulates her brain to support another awesome power—imagination. Through the power of language, children are free to think and talk about what is and what could be. What they see, what they hear, what they want, wonder, and dream about. Of all human gifts, language stands out as infinitely powerful and indispensable. It not only enables us to communicate, but to advance our knowledge; through it we can take advantage of what others have learned. We can envision reality and possibility.

When we use language—to think, speak, and write—we are using symbols: letters and the combinations of letters that make up words. Although we use other kinds of symbols, like numbers, signs, and pictorial images, language is the most widespread symbolic system of communication and the one on which we rely most. Language gives structure to our thoughts. It not only enables us to symbolize objects but to construct entire thoughts and ideas. Our thoughts take shape as an ordered arrangement of words, accompanied by visual imagery, auditory impressions, and feelings.

Language acquisition is a critical part of human development. We begin developing language skills in infancy and early childhood by first understanding spoken language. Then, by copying what we hear, we begin to speak for ourselves. Next, we learn to understand written language—making the connection between spoken words and their printed symbols is the process of learning to read. Finally, we develop the ability to write these symbols ourselves. With reading and writing mastered, we have attained the ultimate reward of language: literacy.

Because of its key role in communication, we tend to think of the importance of reading in terms of enabling us to extract meaning from printed words—to read directions, obtain information, or function in an work environment. However, for our children, the value of reading is more profound. Reading opens them to new experiences: other places, other people, other customs. It enables them to build their knowledge of the world and themselves. It gives them a frame of reference, then moves them beyond their immediate reality to an understanding of a bigger picture.

Reading also stimulates imagination like no other educational or entertainment medium can. If you're an avid reader, you've undoubtedly experienced this pleasure yourself in a book you couldn't put down. Its words fill your mind with images and sensations as fast as the story unfolds. Nothing tops what the mind can see, not even a big-budget Hollywood film. In fact, many a reader has been sorely disappointed by a book brought to the screen. Reading awakens imagination and keeps it alive. Recently, I came across a quote that so eloquently captures the joy of reading that I want to repeat it for you here. The words came from the president of the Carnegie Corporation and former president of the New York Public Library, Dr. Vartan Gregorian: "Any book creates for the reader a place elsewhere. A person reading is a person suspended between the immediate and the timeless. This suspension serves a purpose that has little to do with escaping from the real world, the sin avid readers are most commonly accused of. Reading provides renewal. What is renewed is the imagination."

Even a child being read to experiences this charge of imagination. As she listens, this theater of the mind begins to perform, generating images and impressions, filling in sounds and sensations. Once she learns to read for herself, she can recreate this pleasure independently.

Just as reading exercises imagination, it also limbers and develops our ability to use and manipulate language. The more a child reads, the better he gets at using and manipulating words, the symbols that make up language. Facility with language symbols becomes more important as a child grows up and has to wrestle with abstract thoughts. To think abstractly, we rely on symbols to both formulate thoughts and express them. The more abstract the concept, the more we rely on symbols.

To think abstractly, we also have to be able to organize our thoughts, something most of us don't consciously worry about until we have to put pen to paper, or fingers to keyboard. Because we tend to rely more on conversation to communicate with each other, we're used to a stream-of-consciousness exchange that lets us edit and embellish instantly to express our thoughts. However, when we write, it's a different matter. What we write has to be organized if anyone is to make sense of it. Here, too, reading helps. It reinforces organized thinking because things we read are organized into a beginning, mid-

Reading Myths and Facts

Myth: There is no relationship between TV watching and reading.
Fact: Children who are successful readers watch less TV.

Myth: Any children's television program will help children with vocabulary development.
Fact: Children who watch carefully constructed educational television programs aimed at their age level do better at prereading skills than those children who watch purely entertainment television.

Myth: Children will just naturally learn how to read.
Fact: Children need to be taught to read; their brain development has a big impact on successful reading skills.

Myth: Children's brains develop along a set pattern.
Fact: The development of children's brains responds directly to the environment in which they grow up.

Myth: Reading instruction is a teacher's job and starts in school.
Fact: Parents and other adults can help children have more success with early reading skills if they read to a preschooler, and give that child many experiences with books and print media.

Myth: Children get enough reading practice in school.
Fact: Children need a lot of practice to become fluent readers. Fluent readers read more and enjoy reading more. Television watching can interfere with time a child might spend practicing reading.

Myth: There is no relation between television watching and reading.
Fact: Children who are the heaviest television watchers are also the poorest readers.

Myth: Television watching does not interfere with the quality of homework.
Fact: Television in the background can interfere with the retention of skills and information.

dle, and end. When we read, this discipline rubs off at a sub-conscious level. The more we read, the more proficient we are at using language, thinking abstractly, and writing—of course, this goes for our children, too.

I have long suspected that reading also has a profound effect on another facet of language development: the ability to have a conversation with yourself, or *inner speech*. Inner speech engages critical thinking, allows you to weigh options, consider outcomes, and make decisions based on reasoning. In effect, inner speech helps you to control your impulses: to think before you act. Kids who get into trouble at school for misbehavior are a good example of how impulses work. These kids usually don't premeditate the actions that get them into trouble; they have a problem controlling impulses. Critical thinking doesn't figure in: Inner speech, which would allow them to consider consequences, doesn't happen. Parents and teachers have been saying the same thing to children in these situations for thousands of years: "Think about what you are doing."

Because reading orients us to language, I believe it plays an important part in developing this capability of inner speech. The more I meet with educators, the more I realize I'm not the only one who sees this link. Teachers tell me that the kids who behave most impulsively at school are often poor readers and writers.

Increasingly, studies supporting the importance of reading skills in children are laying it on the line. One of the latest findings concludes that the amount a child reads is the strongest predictor of overall intelligence. Another reveals that children who read the most do the best in a wide variety of academic areas.

With pronouncements like these, it's not surprising that the decline in reading ability is one of the most pressing concerns about children in the United States today. Nationwide, reading scores show that an increasing number of kids cannot read proficiently. In fact, surveys find literacy problems in four out of ten school-age children. Even among adults, there are growing numbers who cannot read well, despite having gone to school. School systems throughout the country are under tremendous pressure to come up with a remedy. Entire school administrations have been removed and replaced as academic scores continue to fall. While it may be true that schools could do a better job of teaching children to read, placing all the blame on school systems or teachers is unfair. In fact, it's a mistake to think that teachers alone are responsible for reading instruction. Studies clearly show that success in reading can begin long before children ever enter the kindergarten classroom.

As you might expect, environmental factors play a critical role in laying a foundation for literacy. Topping the list are family attitudes and behavior: whether a family values and practices reading at home. Timing is critical, too; the early childhood months and years count most. Whether a child is oriented to reading and language during the earliest months and years of development corresponds to success or difficulty with reading in school. As a parent, this means you have tremendous power. Getting your child off on the right foot with reading begins with you and the earlier you intervene the better. If your child is older, all is not lost; but the job of turning a child onto reading does get harder the longer you wait. Later in this chapter, we'll look at strategies for encouraging reading in older children and changing habits that get in the way. If you're inclined to skip ahead to find out what's in store for you, hold off. The next few pages will give you an understanding of how children develop a pattern of reading success or difficulty, and what factors reinforce these patterns. With these insights in mind, you'll be prepared to put solutions to work in your family.

If you have an infant, preschooler, or early elementary student at home, studies have identified a number of experiences you can provide to position your child for reading success:

1. Engage your child in language. Talk with her a lot, even before she's able to speak. Tell her about her world, what things are, what she sees and hears, what she's doing, what you're doing. Because children learn to speak by copying the language they hear, they need talkative role models. Once your child begins to talk, engage her in conversation. Encourage her to label objects and help her with vocabulary and pronunciation. Reinforce her efforts by responding and praising her ability.

2. Read to your child every day. This is one of the most important preliteracy activities you can do with your child. Even before their first birthday, children commonly have a favorite book and can recognize books on sight. By reading to your child, you help him begin to associate reading with pleasure.

3. Create a reading environment. Show the importance of reading in your family by having lots of reading material around—books, magazines, newspapers. Arrange your living space so that it encourages reading: comfortable places to cuddle up together with a book, good lighting, easy-access shelves, or baskets of books. Orient your reading environment to focus on the available reading materials rather than on a television set; reposition your TV so that it is not the center of attention.

4. Model reading behavior. Let your child see how important reading is to you by doing it yourself. Expose him to the importance and ritual of reading by visiting the library.

By orienting children to reading early on, these experiences establish reading as a positive, enjoyable goal. This is invaluable groundwork to lay before it comes time to learn to read in school. Reading skills take time to develop. Very few children pick up the ability to read quickly; the same goes for learning to write proficiently. For most kids, learning to read requires effort and, for some, a great deal of effort. In turn, the benefits of reading aren't immediately available; gratification is delayed until you have the skill. So, children who have been given an early, consistent orientation to reading come into the learning process that many steps ahead: They come with reinforced interest and positive expectations. They are more likely to hang in there as their skills slowly develop, and are more likely to succeed sooner at acquiring the reading skills they need to experience the rewards. Once they get a taste of the reward, they're hooked and the cycle of success feeds itself. Kids who get better at reading get more enjoyment from it and are more motivated to do it; the more motivated they are to do it, the better they become.

The reverse is also true. Kids who have more trouble with reading get frustrated quickly and begin to associate reading with personal failure. Naturally, they avoid it. Of course, if they avoid reading they aren't practicing it and aren't improving. So, when they do read, they're all the more frustrated and less willing to put in the time they need. It's easy to see how a cycle of defeat builds momentum. The gap between kids with reading skills and those without them develops quickly.

A recent study of kids' reading habits outside school emphasizes this phenomenon. The study found that kids who read at the ninety-eighth percentile read on average sixty-five minutes a day outside school. From this high the numbers drop off quickly: kids reading at the fiftieth percentile (the average reader) read only 4.6 minutes a day outside school; kids at the twentieth percentile and below read less than a minute a day outside school. To look at it another way, a kid who reads sixty-five minutes a day outside of school will have read 4,358,000 words over the course of a year. A kid who reads only 4.6 minutes a day will have read 282,000 words in a year. For parents whose kids have trouble reading, these are tough statistics to face. We have to wonder if society can afford this kind of gap. How will growing numbers of children who can't read proficiently eventually be able to meet the demands of an increasingly competitive economy?

Now that you have reading with a capital R under your skin, it's time to look at how media figures in. A good starting point is the well-worn fact you've encountered throughout this book: that the average child in the United States spends more time watching TV and using other forms of media than doing any other activity in his or her waking life. So, take a look at how your family spends their free time and think about what it means. In light of what we know about the importance of prereading experiences and the rich-get-richer reading syndrome, you could say that where media is concerned, the writing is on the wall.

For kids who are learning to read, the problem isn't so much what they're doing when they watch TV and play video games, but what they're not doing (and how much they're not doing it) that takes a toll on the development of literacy skills. In the early school years, when kids spend a lot of time watching TV or playing video games, critical reading time is being displaced, and this displacement is habit forming. By nature, TV and other visual media offer instant gratification: No advance preparation is required, no effort is needed, anyone can do it. TV is much easier to understand and become engaged in than reading. So, avid watching or game playing reinforces a pattern of instant gratification—a dangerous situation for kids who find learning to read difficult. These are the kids who need practice reading the most.

For them, a habit of watching television becomes a habit of seeking the path of least resistance. Faced with competing activities—reading, which brings some frustration, or watching television and playing video games, which is instantly rewarding—the more enjoyable option wins out. When these kids get to school and have to work on reading, they become more frustrated; not only have they avoided the reading practice they need, they're also accustomed to the instant payoff of entertainment media, and are less willing to work for the rewards of reading. So, more and more they turn to media for entertainment and stimulation. At the same time, they get farther and farther away from any hope of improving their reading skills. The research to support this sad fact is unwavering: The more a child watches TV, the lower his or her reading scores. In fact, kids who participate in media entertainment (TV, video games) for more than two hours a day don't do as well in reading or school in general.

On a more positive note, research also shows that reading and academic scores are unaffected in kids who watch a moderate amount of TV (less than one to two hours a day). Some studies indicate that a moderate amount of educational programming may be a positive force for young readers and help them do well in school. Certain programs, like *Sesame Street* and *Between the Lions*, can actually help develop literacy skills in young children. In general, however, the media diet for preschoolers and early elementary students should be limited. When they do watch television, the best options are educational programs, especially those that introduce reading skills and the rewards that go with language and literacy. If you need help narrowing the field, search your TV listing for shows labeled E/I for educational/instructional (for more on the E/I symbol, see chapter 4). Then, preview the options to be sure they offer the educational value you're seeking.

For parents who worry that they've missed the boat on reading now that their child is nine, twelve, or sixteen, rest assured that there is hope. You and your child have some work cut out for you; it's time to give reading another chance. Even if your child hasn't picked up a book in eons, together you can make reading more fun and more important in your family. That you work on this together is essential. Once a habit of not reading is *status quo,* your child has developed very specific ideas about what is more fun and more worthwhile than reading—like watching television, or playing video and computer games.

You have to make changes in small steps. Imagine the response you'd get if you did away with the TV, boxed up all the video games, and demanded three hours of book time a night. The key is to draw your child into a plan by making reading an attractive alternative to zoning out in front of the tube, or whiling away hours at the computer. Here are some strategies to get you going:

1. Make reading attractive. From the arrangement of your furniture to the availability of reading materials, make reading look important and inviting in your home. Have things to read that will be especially interesting to your child—a story about a place he'd like to go, a book about a subject she loves, an article about an event he's looking forward to.

2. Give your child a reason to read. Giving your child a reason to read is more than half the battle. Whether it's joining a community soccer team, signing up for riding lessons, starting a hobby, or taking care of a new puppy, give your child something to be excited about—and something to read about. Look for age-appropriate reading materials on the subject: books, magazine articles, paperback stories. Encourage your child to talk about what she's read, and involve her in choosing additional reading materials.

3. Replace media little by little with attractive alternatives. By getting your child involved in activities that he'll think are fun (at least as fun as watching TV), you'll begin to whittle away at his media diet. With his input, plan outings, sign up for lessons, begin a project together—anything enjoyable that takes the focus (and time) away from media. Then find opportunities to link reading to the activity. Remember, the idea is to gradually work in alternatives to media. As your child learns to look forward to doing something else on a regular basis, not only will he get used to that much less media

time, he may begin seeking alternatives on his own—and when he does, be ready to encourage him.

4. Make reading a family pleasure. Set aside time as a family to read for fun. Read about something the whole family is interested in and link it to a reward. For example, read about different places to take a family vacation, then plan a trip. Or turn a family event into an opportunity to do some reading on the subject: getting a pet, building a darkroom, visiting a museum exhibit.

5. Record your child's story. Make your own book by inviting your child to tell a story about himself (or anything he'd like) while you write it down. Let him illustrate the story by drawing, pasting in photographs, or cutting out pictures from magazines. This not only gives you something special to read together, but reinforces the joy of storytelling.

6. Select media products that promote reading. When your child does play computer games, choose programs that incorporate reading skills and problem solving into the fun. Also, look for video rentals that include a book component.

7. Make deals that both of you can live with. Work out an agreement that she gets to play her video game if she plays a reading-related video game first. Or, he gets to watch his TV program (one you approve of, of course) if he reads something first; recording a favorite show is a good way to avoid the inevitable time conflict.

Raising literate children should be an issue for all parents, whether their children are not yet in school or well on the way. Getting involved in your child's reading life is one of the most important commitments you will ever undertake, however old she is. You are your child's best chance for success. If we, as a culture, want to reverse the decline in literacy that is plaguing our children, we, as parents, need to look at what our children are doing before they ever set foot in a classroom. If media is gobbling up so much of their time that they aren't getting the orientation to language and reading they will need when they get to school, they are missing out on something school can't easily make up for: reading as a family value, reading as a pleasure and an adventure, reading as a goal. We know that kids who read well do better in school across the board. Kids who have a positive orientation to reading early on are more likely to want to do it later, to stay with it, and figure it out, to realize the rewards. Children who get a later start in reading need all the more attention and encouragement to keep from falling between the cracks. Whether it happens sooner or later, an orientation to reading begins at home. Children need to experience reading on a regular basis among the people they are with the most. When reading has a significant place in our families, we set something priceless in motion for our children. We open the doors to something lasting, something they will build on, depend on, and enjoy for the rest of their lives. And in the process we also preserve something great and irreplaceable: their imagination.

Extending the Cyberhood Map

Now that we have seen how important literacy is, let's turn to some activities that will help translate that into action. First, an activity designed to help you figure out how reading friendly your home is. The next three activities provide plenty of ideas for resources to track down the kinds of books kids will love, as well as how to link electronic media into the process and tips for raising readers. The concluding activity will help you pull it all together into an action plan.

CHAPTER TEN ACTIVITIES

Activity: Reading Checklist

For parents.

This inventory will help you take a quick measure of the reading environment in your home.

At the start of each age category, you will see three traffic signs:

Go   **Caution**   **Stop**

For each age category that applies to your family, circle the answers that describe your family's reading habits.

In each column Y is Yes; S, Sometimes; and N, No.

GETTING READY TO READ MEASURE

Preschool children
Think about the time your preschool child spends with books.

	Go	Caution	Stop
Does your child have books geared to her/his age?	Y	S	N
Does your child visit the library to look at books, hear stories, and so on?	Y	S	N

	Y	S	N
Does someone read to your child every day?	Y	S	N
Does your child watch you read for fun or information?	Y	S	N
Is your child learning the alphabet?	Y	S	N
Do you and your child talk about a story or an activity that you share each day?	Y	S	N
When your child watches TV, is the program an educational program made for preschool children?	Y	S	N

Elementary age reader
Think about the time your elementary-age child spends reading.

	Go	Caution	Stop
Does your child do homework with the television on?	N	S	Y
Does your child have a library card and use it?	Y	S	N
Does your home have a quiet reading space?	Y	S	N
Does your child have access to sources of information at home, like books, magazines, computer, and the Internet?	Y	S	N

•   •   •   •   •   •   •   •   •   •   •

	Y	S	N
Do you read to your child (picture books or chapter books)?	Y	S	N
Does your child spend time reading every day?	Y	S	N

Middle- and high-school reader
Think about the time your older child spends reading.

	Go	Caution	Stop
Do you ever buy your older child a book or magazine?	Y	S	N
Does your child do homework with the TV on?	N	S	Y
Do you talk about ideas that you have read about?	Y	S	N
Does your child have access to reference materials at home?	Y	S	N
Does your child see you read for pleasure?	Y	S	N
Does your child have a comfortable, quiet place to read?	Y	S	N

Scoring: Look at your answers for each category.

Answers circled in the **Go** (green-light) column indicate that your family has a supportive reading environment.

Answers circled in the **Caution** (yellow-light) column indicate that you might want to take time to review your family's reading habits in that area.

•   •   •   •   •   •   •   •   •   •   •

Answers circled in the **Stop** (red-light) column indicate that you might want to think about changing your family's reading habits in these areas.

Children's Book Awards

Every year, many organizations single out one or more children's books or authors for special recognition. Some of these awards are made on the basis of the content of a story, others on the basis of the beauty of the illustrations. For whatever reason, these awards highlight some of the best children's literature in any given year. The following are some of the most respected awards:

1. These awards are presented annually by the American Library Association:

The *Coretta Scott King Award.* Since 1982, this award has been given to African-American authors and illustrators whose noted books promote understanding and achievement. This award highlights the work of Dr. Martin Luther King and his widow, Coretta Scott King. A recent winner is *Bud, Not Buddy* by Christopher Paul Curtis.

The *Caldecott Medal.* This award is given annually to an artist for the best illustrations in a children's book. Awarded since 1938, the Caldecott Medal is named after Randolph Caldecott, a nineteen-century English illustrator. The committee may also award Caldecott Honor books in any given year, for those books that are also distinguished by their illustrations. *Joseph Had a Little Overcoat* by Simms Taback is a recent winner.

The *Newbery Medal*. The Newbery Medal is given annually to an author of a distinguished children's literature book. Here, the committee is looking at content and this award is usually given for books aimed at older elementary and middle-school children. Named for eighteenth-century British bookseller, John Newbery, this award has been given since 1922. The committee may also award Newbery Honor books in any given year. *Bud, Not Buddy* by Christopher Paul Curtis is a recent winner.

2. The Consortium of Latin American Studies Programs presents the *Americas Award for Children's and Young Adult Literature*. Each year since 1993, a book is chosen which authentically portrays the experience of living in the Caribbean or Latin America, or the experience of a Latino in the United States. Honor books are also listed. Recent winners include *Barrio: Jose's Neighborhood: El Barrio De Jose* by George Ancona and *Mama and Papa Have a Store* by Amelia Carling.

3. The *Boston Globe–Horn Book Award*. Since 1967 the *Boston Globe* and the *Horn Book Magazine* have teamed together to present an award to outstanding children's picture books and fiction or poetry books. A nonfiction category was added in 1976. Recent winners have been *Holes* by Louis Sachar (fiction/poetry); *The Top of the World: Climbing Mount Everest* by Steve Jenkins (nonfiction); and *Red-Eyed Tree Frog* by Nic Bishop (children's picture book).

4. *The National Book Award for Young People's Literature* is awarded annually to an outstanding children's or young adult book written by an American author. *When Zachary Beaver Came to Town* by Kimberly Willis Holt is a recent winner in the young-adult category.

5. The *Golden Kite Award* of the Society of Children's Book Writers and Illustrators is the only award selected by

writers and illustrators. Awards are given in the picture book, fiction, nonfiction, and illustrators' categories. Among the recent winners are *Rules of the Road* by Joan Bauer (fiction); *Martha Graham: A Dancer's Life* by Russell Freedman (nonfiction); *Old Elm Speaks* by Kristine O'Connell George (picture book); and *Snow* by Uri Shulevitz (illustration).

6. Three awards are given by the Children's Book Committee at Bank Street College for books that deal "realistically and in a positive way with problems in their world." Recent winners have been *My Louisiana Sky* by Kimberly Willis Holt; *Iqbal Masih and the Crusaders Against Child Slavery* by Susan Kuklin; and *I, Too, Sing America* by Catherine Clinton.

7. The Christophers have given the *Christopher Award* to works in the young people's category "which affirm the highest values of the human spirit." A recent winner was *Raising Dragons* by Jerdine Nolen, illustrated by Elise Primavera.

8. The National Council of Teachers of English each year presents the *Orbis Pictus Award* for a distinctive work of nonfiction for children. This award was established in 1990 and is named after *Orbis Pictus*, published in 1657 and considered to be the first informational book ever written for children. *Shipwreck at the Bottom of the World* by Jennifer Armstrong is a recent winner.

9. The *Jane Addams Children's Book Award* is given by the Women's International League for Peace and Freedom and the Jane Addams Peace Association. The award is for books that best promote peace, understanding, and social justice in the world community. *Bat 6* by Virginia Euwer Wolff in the young adult category and *Painted Words/Spoken Memories* by Akiki in the picture-book category are recent winners.

10. The *Giverny Award* was first presented in the spring of 1998 to the outstanding children's science book of the year by

scientists at the 15 Degree Laboratory at Louisiana State University. *Sam Plants a Sunflower* by Katte Petty and Axel Scheffler is a recent winner.

Media Resources to Promote Reading

Television programs, World Wide Web sites, and children's magazines are great resources for helping children become better readers. Here are some suggestions in each category.

Television

Your public television station is an excellent resource for programs that help children to read. Here are some of the programs:

- *Sesame Street.* This classic children's program teaches preschoolers many basic literacy skills. (Preschool)
- *Storytime.* A combination of puppets and live guests introduce children to the world of books. (Preschool)
- *Reading Rainbow.* Host LeVar Burton leads children on an engaging adventure, then reads a picture book on the same theme. Children also recommend their favorite books, which gives the viewer a great list of interesting books. (Elementary)
- *Arthur.* This series is based on the many Arthur books by Marc Brown. (Elementary)
- *Wishbone.* Children get an introduction to classical literature, as Wishbone the dog bridges the gap be-

tween real life and that of many classic stories. (Elementary)

- *Between the Lions* This program teaches letters, sounds, and words to the elementary-school-age child. (Elementary)

Many cable channels also have shows that are based on children's books:

- *HBO Storybook Musicals.* These HBO specials present animated musical stories based on favorite children's books like *Alexander and the Terrible, Horrible, No Good, Very Bad Day.* (Preschool)
- *The Busy World of Richard Scarry* is on Nickelodeon and Showtime. This is an animated series combining music and short stories, based on the books by Richard Scarry. (Preschool)
- *Happily Ever After: Fairy Tales for Every Child* is on HBO. This is an animated series based on popular fairy tales. (Elementary)

There are many other educational shows on public television and other cable networks like the Discovery Channel, Animal Planet, Nickelodeon, the Disney Channel, and the History Channel. These programs may spur a child to want to read further about the topic of the program.

The Internet

There are many World Wide Web sites that offer parents support with reading resources, and offer children either information or an opportunity to interact with their favorite author or get information about their favorite books. Here are some of the best sites on the web.

For parents:

- *The Children's Literature WEB Guide.* This is one of the best resources on the Internet for information about children's and young-adult books. Check here for award winners, authors, illustrators, book-discussion groups, and book lists.
  http://www.acs.ucalgary.cal/~dkbrown/index.html
- *Fairrosa Cyber Library of Children's Literature.* This site provides links to other resources on the web, such as online books and authors' websites.
  http://www.users.interport.net/~fairrosa/
- *American Library Association's Resource for Parents and Kids.* You'll find information here on Caldecott and Newbery award-winning books as well as links to other sites.
  http://www.ala.org/parents/index.html

For children:

- *Internet Public Library Youth Division.* You can read story hour selections, information about authors, and much more at this cyber library.
  http://www.ipl.org/youth/
- *Middle School Book Review Website.* Kids from all over the country share their reviews of their favorite books. Children can add their own reviews or pick out a title that looks interesting.
  http://www.xrds.org/xrds/BookReviews/intro.html
- *Yahoo!* This portal and search engine offers a children's author site with links to the web pages of a multitude of children's book authors.
  http://www.yahoo.com/Arts/Humanities/Literature/
  Genres/Childrens/Authors/

Magazines

There are many children's magazines on the market. Some of these magazines are mere vehicles to place more advertising in front of your child; many others showcase wonderful children's literature or encourage them to read more about topics that interest them. Listed here is a sample of magazines that will invite your child into the world of reading:

- Cobblestone Publishers have created a number of award-winning magazines aimed at children ages seven to fourteen. With an emphasis on history, the nonfiction content introduces children to a rich variety of people, places and events. (Call 1-800-821-0115.)

  Cobblestone. American history.

  Footsteps. African-American heritage.

  Faces. People, places, and culture.

  Odyssey. Adventures in science.

  Appleseeds. For children ages seven through nine.
- Cricket Magazines produces magazines for children ages six months and up. With an emphasis on fiction, these stories, poems, and songs engage the imagination of every child. (Call 1-800-827-0227 for information.)

  Babybug. Simple rhymes and stories for the youngest child, ages six months to two years.

  Ladybug. A highly illustrated magazine for the pre-schooler, ages two and up.

  Spider. For the beginning reader, ages six and up.

  Cricket. Stories of high interest and adventure, along with puzzles and games for the reader, ages nine and up.

  Cicada. For the teen reader, ages fourteen and up.

• *MUSE* is a magazine produced by Cricket Publications sponsored by the Smithsonian Museum for ages eight to fourteen. It is a nonfiction magazine on topics ranging from art to zoology, all based on the museum's collections and research. (Call 1-800-827-0227 for information.)

• *New Moon: The Magazine for Girls and Their Dreams.* This magazine is edited by girls ages eight to fourteen, and has contributors from all over the world. Its aim is to celebrate girls and give voice to their concerns and interests. (Call 1-800-381-4743 for information.)

• The National Wildlife Federation sponsors two magazines for children. (Call 1-800-611-1599 for information.)

   Ranger Rick. This magazine is packed with information, colorful photos, stories, and games aimed at fostering environmental awareness among elementary-age children.

   Your Big Backyard. This highly illustrated nature magazine is aimed at three- to six-year-olds.

• *Stone Soup.* This magazine is written and illustrated by children ages eight to thirteen from all over the world. (Call 1-800-447-4569 for information.)

Your Local Library

Your local library is a great resource. Make sure your child has a library card. Don't hesitate to ask your librarian about books and other materials that might interest your child. Many libraries sponsor summer reading programs; most have story hours for preschoolers.

Activity: Tips for Raising Readers

For parents.

Reading offers many rewards for parents and children. Children will be more successful in school if they are read to or read on their own at least twenty minutes every day.

Reading to Your Baby or Toddler

It's never too early to start reading to your child. Very young children love the rhythmic language of nursery rhymes and the bright pictures in books geared to their age level. Don't be surprised if your child would rather eat the book, or cannot sit still for more than a few seconds or a few pages. Don't give up. Just enjoy the time with them.

Cuddling, sitting the child on your lap, or right next to you, gives a strong emotional support for reading. Follow your child's interest. Let them turn the pages. Don't be surprised if they insist on turning three at a time!

Choose a board book or picture book that has simple pictures and uncluttered pages. Have a conversation with your child, pointing out and naming pictures and relating them to the child's own life.

With a picture book, don't worry about the text, just talk to your child about the pictures. If you are reading a nursery-rhyme book, give expression to the language. Act it out. Use descriptive words to indicate color (brown dog), size (big ball), location (a truck under the table or next to a chair), and so on.

Ask them questions about the picture. (Where's the ball? What does a cow say? Here's an arm, where is Erin's arm?)

Don't expect your child to finish a book. When they are bored, tired, or just ready to do something else, stop.

Keep your reading time short, but do it every day.

Did something strike you as important about reading to your baby or toddler? Write it down here:

_____

_____

_____

Reading to Your Younger Child

The importance of reading aloud to your child cannot be overemphasized. Create a space at home for books and reading. Sit close together in a comfy spot. Encourage questions and verbal interactions about what you are reading. Elaborate on the story. Ask your child about what they think will happen. Be a storyteller with a wordless book. Or, let your child tell a story about the pictures.

Continue to read more difficult books out loud with your child. Don't be afraid to read a longer chapter book to your child. Reading a book with few pictures, once in a while, helps activate your child's imagination. You will want to read just a short segment, stopping before a child loses interest. Your local librarian or children's bookstore will have good suggestions for chapter books that are fun to read aloud. Or visit our website at www.mediafamily.org, click on Free Family Resources, and then on Dr. Dave's Family Favorites. Find the list that suggests favorite read-aloud books.

Visit the library with your child. Take part in story hours. As your child begins to learn to read, help them practice reading aloud at home. Make reading a part of everyday activities. Plan a small garden with your child. Read together about seeds and planting instructions. Encourage questions. If you don't know the answers, look up information in a book or on the Internet. Encourage your child to read recipes for simple cooking projects.

Did something strike you as important about reading to your preschool or early elementary child? Write it down here:

_____

_____

_____

For the Older Child

There are many things you can do to encourage your middle-grade or high-school student to read. Have a space in your home and in your child's bedroom for books, and comfortable, well-lit places for reading. Include some reference books or computer programs in your home library (i.e., dictionary, almanac, encyclopedia, thesaurus).

Talk at dinner about what you have read in a book or magazine.

Don't forget to buy a book for your child. (If you buy video or computer games, your child will see value in books if you also buy them as presents.) Key in to your child's interests. Buy fiction and nonfiction. Give a gift certificate to your local bookstore so your child can pick out her own books.

If your child is a reluctant reader, casually introduce a magazine or book about a topic in which they are interested. A book at first rejected may be picked up later. Some children who do not read many books may enjoy reading magazines. Some children are interested only in nonfiction books, others will read only fiction.

Your child may still enjoy your reading longer chapter books aloud, or they may enjoy reading to you. Some older children may still enjoy a picture book by their favorite author.

Make sure your child has a library card and an opportunity to visit the library.

Continue to make reading a part of everyday activities. If you have to assemble something, have your child read you the instructions and help put it together. Encourage your child to do projects where they have to read instructions and figure out how to accomplish a task. Cooking (even instructions on microwaving) is another area that can involve reading.

Did something strike you as important about reading and your middle-grade child or teenager? Write it down here:

_____

_____

_____

Activity: Plan for Raising Readers

For parents.

This activity contains many different strategies that you can use to encourage your children to read and write. They are broken down according to age. You will notice that some of them appear on all the lists; that's because they work with children of any age. Others are more age specific. Use the list to gather some new ideas, and also to create an action plan for raising readers.

1. Find the section that matches the ages of your children.
2. Answer the question according to the following scale: 1, never; 2, sometimes; 3, often; 4, always.
3. Circle the items that you think are the most helpful for you.
4. At the end, choose the three you want to either start or increase and write them down. This becomes your action plan for raising readers.

For babies and toddlers

1. Do you talk a lot to your baby?   1   2   3   4
2. Do you help her label objects?   1   2   3   4
3. Do you praise your baby's language abilities?   1   2   3   4
4. As your child begins to talk, do you praise his questions?   1   2   3   4
5. Do you buy your baby books?   1   2   3   4
6. Do you encourage others to buy your baby books as presents?   1   2   3   4
7. Do you read to your baby?   1   2   3   4
8. Do you let your baby turn the pages?   1   2   3   4
9. Do you make reading an interactive experience by asking questions and making remarks?   1   2   3   4

10. Do you read your baby's favorite book as often as they want, even after you're tired of reading it? 1 2 3 4

11. Do you have reading materials around the house? 1 2 3 4

12. Are there paper, pencils, and crayons easily available? 1 2 3 4

13. Does your baby see you reading? 1 2 3 4

14. Do you encourage your older children to read to the baby? 1 2 3 4

15. Do you have a comfy spot for reading to your baby? 1 2 3 4

16. Do you have a ritual of reading a bedtime story? 1 2 3 4

17. Do you display their early drawings in a prominent place? 1 2 3 4

18. Do you keep a reading diary of the books your baby enjoyed as a baby so he can see it when he is older. 1 2 3 4

For preschool and early-elementary age children

1. Do you talk a lot with your children? 1 2 3 4

2. Do you turn the TV off during meals to encourage conversation? 1 2 3 4

3. Do you have a lot of books, magazines, and newspapers around? 1 2 3 4

4. Is the room arranged to encourage reading with good lighting, comfortable chairs? 1 2 3 4

5. Do your children see you reading? 1 2 3 4

6. Do you read billboards, street signs, and package labels out loud? 1 2 3 4

7. Do your children receive books as gifts? 1 2 3 4

8. Do you have plenty of age-appropriate reading materials around? 1 2 3 4

9. Do you read stories out loud to your children? 1 2 3 4

10. Do you read your child's favorite books as often as they want even if you have grown tired of it? 1 2 3 4

11. Do you listen to books on tape during car rides? 1 2 3 4

12. Do you have reading materials that match your child's interests? 1 2 3 4

13. Do you look for TV programs that encourage reading? 1 2 3 4

14. Do you buy video and computer games that encourage reading? 1 2 3 4

15. Do you take your children to the library? 1 2 3 4

16. Do you encourage your older children to read to the younger ones? 1 2 3 4

17. Do you leave a good supply of books for the baby-sitter? 1 2 3 4

18. Do you take your children to the children's section of bookstores? 1 2 3 4

19. Do you read about places you will be visiting? 1 2 3 4

20. Do you keep a reading diary of your children's favorite books? 1 2 3 4

21. Do you write stories that your children   1 2 3 4
    dictate?

22. Do you display you children's drawings   1 2 3 4
    and art work in a prominent place?

23. Do you limit the time your children   1 2 3 4
    spend watching TV, videos, and electronic
    games?

24. Do you make deals that involve reading,   1 2 3 4
    for example, you can watch TV after you
    spend some time reading? (Don't use
    books as a threat.)

For middle-elementary and middle-school years

1. Do you talk a lot with your children?   1 2 3 4

2. Do you turn the TV off during meals to   1 2 3 4
   encourage conversation?

3. Do you have a lot of books, magazines,   1 2 3 4
   and newspapers around?

4. Is the room arranged to encourage   1 2 3 4
   reading, with good lighting, and comfort-
   able chairs?

5. Do your children see you reading?   1 2 3 4

6. Do your children receive books as gifts?   1 2 3 4

7. Do you have plenty of age-appropriate   1 2 3 4
   reading materials around?

8. Do you still read stories out loud to your   1 2 3 4
   children?

9. Do you listen to books on tape during   1 2 3 4
   car rides?

10. Do you have reading materials that match   1 2 3 4
    your child's interests?

11. Do you look for TV programs that   1 2 3 4
    encourage reading?

12. Do you buy video and computer games   1 2 3 4
    that encourage reading?

13. Does your child have a library card?   1 2 3 4

14. Do you encourage them to read to   1 2 3 4
    younger children?

15. Do you read about places you will be   1 2 3 4
    visiting?

16. Do you display your child's writing in a   1 2 3 4
    prominent place?

17. Do you limit TV, video, and video-game   1 2 3 4
    time?

18. Do you make deals that involve reading,   1 2 3 4
    for example, you can watch TV after you
    spend some time reading? (Don't use
    books as a threat.)

For teenagers

1. Do you talk a lot with your teens?   1 2 3 4

2. Do you turn the TV off during meals to   1 2 3 4
   encourage conversation?

3. Do you have a lot of books, magazines,   1 2 3 4
   and newspapers around?

4. Is the room arranged to encourage   1 2 3 4
   reading, with good lighting, and comfort-
   able chairs?

5. Do your teenagers see you reading? 1 2 3 4

6. Do your teenagers receive books as gifts? 1 2 3 4

7. Do you listen to books on tape during car rides? 1 2 3 4

8. Do you have reading materials that match your child's interests? 1 2 3 4

9. Do you buy video and computer games that involve a lot of reading? 1 2 3 4

10. Do you point out articles in newspapers or magazines that you think your teen might be interested in? 1 2 3 4

11. Do you encourage them to read to younger children? 1 2 3 4

12. Do you still display their written work (essays, tests) in a prominent place? 1 2 3 4

13. Have you ever thought of organizing a parent/child book club? 1 2 3 4

14. Do you clip articles about movies or musical performers that they are interested in? 1 2 3 4

15. Do you suggest that they read a book and then watch the movie version to decide which is better? 1 2 3 4

The three steps that I will take to do a better job of raising readers are:

1. _____

2. _____

3. _____

CHAPTER ELEVEN

• • • • • • • • • • •

Conclusion: Peering into the Cyberfuture

By now, you have collected, sorted, sifted, and weighed more ideas about media than you ever have dreamed could be part of parenthood. For better and worse, media's potential to affect children gives parents a lot to think about and a lot to do. If, at times, the task awaiting you has seemed overwhelming, my hope is that now you feel empowered by your responsibility, confident that you can have a say in the role of media in your child's life, and certain that you should. In providing you with information, strategies, and resolve, this book has also done something else: It has prepared you to look ahead at what parenting in an age of media will mean five, seven, and ten years from now, for you will face a dramatically different landscape all over again. Just as you've had to adapt your caregiving to meet the challenges of today's media-saturated world, the evolution of technology will insist that you continue to adapt before your job is done. If you feel a bit insecure at the prospect of yet another learning curve, hear this: You are ahead of the game. Right now, you are in a prime position to understand the implications of media's future. When the time comes to adapt to the next wave of challenges, you will be ready. You will recognize the importance of managing your child's media diet, and be able to build on what you've already learned. You will know how to step in, set limits, and define ground rules—and you will have the clarity to stand firm in your vision of media's place in your child's life.

This final chapter will give you a glimpse of media to come, and a taste of what the changes will mean for children and families. It is an appropriate conclusion to the book, but it is also an important beginning for you and every caregiver in the media age. These last few pages underscore the importance of your commitment to managing your child's media diet, not just for today, but *because* of tomorrow.

If we look into the crystal ball of media's future, three potent forces surface in the cyberfog: the convergence, commercialization, and entertainmentization of media. While none of these phenomena are new, they will intensify, overlap, and reinforce each other in the next decade. They will become inseparable, together creating a new breed of media: *convergent commertainment*. This new hybrid form of media promises to be even more powerful, more omnipresent, more integrated into the lives of our children than all the media we live with today. And, true to the pace of technological change, this next media revolution won't be long in coming. In fact, it already has a foothold in reality.

Convergent Commertainment

On November 1, 1998, digital television signals were broadcast for the first time in history. This milestone event officially launched media, as we know it, into a new era. Yet, most viewers in America aren't even sure what digital TV is, let alone aware of its implications. Digital TV, as you may have guessed, does refer to *high definition TV* (HDTV), which gives us clearer, sharper pictures. While picture quality is an inherent capability of digital TV, it's just the tip of the electronic iceberg. The conversion from analog to digital television raises TV's communication ability to a powerful, new level. In digital format, television signals can now speak the same language as other important forms of media communication: computers at work and at home, the Internet, cell phones. As all media forms convert to digital format, the lines that separate them will be erased. Media as separate entities will disappear, and re-emerge as a *converged* species, a single appliance, technologically integrated, pulsing with the same life blood: digital information.

This new media will seamlessly integrate our televisions, telephones, faxes, and computers. We'll be able to watch TV, play video games, answer the phone, listen to CDs, send an e-mail, and surf the Internet via a single communication source. Instead of dozens of channels now available on cable TV, or hundreds of options via satellite, the convergence of the Internet with television will provide *thousands* of choices. In the age of new media, any website will have the potential to become a global television network.

It's mind-boggling to realize how close this transformation is to becoming part of our everyday lives. With televisions and telephones already converging in the great lab of technology, video telephones are likely to fill store shelves in a matter of seasons. A child in diapers today will be able to experience widespread media convergence by the time he's in grade school. He'll be able to sit on the family-room couch, thumb on a remote, and click effortlessly and seamlessly from a TV program to a video game to a video on demand to a World Wide Web site to telephone communication to downloading documents from a home computer. That's not all. Via layering technology, he'll also be able to interact with the images he sees onscreen. Let's say he's watching a nature program, and wants to know more about a volcano in the background. All he has to do is *click* and voilà, supplemental video and text appear in the corner of the screen. In the meantime, the rest of the program will continue, so he doesn't have to miss a thing; like that cool T-shirt the nature guide is wearing. Where *did* he get it? *Click.* Oh, look, it's available for purchase in his size, delivery guaranteed in twenty-four to forty-eight hours. With this kind of interactivity at our fingertips, watching television in the coming years will take on a whole new meaning for everyone in the family.

Along with the marvels of convergence, other technological developments promise to reinforce the power of new media. Major advances in image and sound technology are moving us ever closer to that Hollywood-manufactured phenomenon, virtual reality. As greater and greater amounts of video and audio information can be transmitted at higher and higher speeds, the quality of pictures, graphics, and sounds will approach real-life quality. What we see onscreen in our own homes will be as clear and sharp as what we can see across a room. What we hear onscreen will be as immediate and authentic as your voice calling from the next room. Combined with technical capabilities like these, the choices, layers, and seamless interactivity of convergence, will make for a media world that is much more engaging, realistic, and engrossing than anything we experience today.

Exactly what this new media will look like is still a mystery but, what is certain is that, over the next ten years, the world of media will bring about a cultural revolution every bit as profound as the transition from radio to television. The other thing we can count on is that new media will be the way of life for our youngest generation of children as they grow up. By the very nature of convergence, new media will become an even bigger part of their experience than current media is for kids today. And children of the new media age will adapt as easily to its power as present generations have to the media with which we live today.

If we have any doubts that such awesome change is near, we have only to look at how major media businesses are investing their wealth and reshaping their potential. Broadcast television is investing in cable. Long-distance giants are buying up local cable companies. Every major TV network is investing in Internet portals in anticipation of powerful opportunities in the era of digital convergence; because users must return repeatedly to portals in order to maneuver the Internet, businesses that control these entry points to cyberspace have automatic and concentrated access to potential customers worldwide. Companies are also hedging their bets to take advantage of whichever pipeline wins out as the most cost-effective and efficient carrier of digital information: telephone lines, cable lines, satellite, or direct high-capacity fiberoptic lines. Some companies are already joining forces to dabble in the possibilities of convergence. MSNBC Cable is the result of one such joint venture between media superpowers: Microsoft, one of most powerful drivers of the digital economy, and NBC, one of the giants of television broadcasting, have teamed up to deliver their messages through cable. The AOL/Time Warner and the ATT/Media One mergers are further indications of convergence. These and others like these show that joint ventures and crossfertilizations will become common.

The second major force certain to shape the new media environment is commercialization. As we know, the pairing of commercial interests and media is nothing new. For more than two hundred years of media evolution this union has proven stunningly successful. Now, in the era of Internet communication, history has begun to repeat itself, but with even greater promise of wedded bliss for the happy couple. Just a few years ago, the Internet was a communication network for scientists and researchers; commercial sites were unheard of. With the turn of the millennium, the numbers of commercial sites are uncountable.

In the new media age, the blending of commerce and media will be complete and profound. Until now, media has been primarily a tool for marketing and advertising. The commercial interest of television, for example, has been to deliver eyeballs to advertisers. With the exception of home shopping, television commerce has been a one-way experience, an advertiser's effort to communicate its message to you. To act on a decision to buy, you have had to go elsewhere: to a grocery store, a shopping mall, an auto dealer. In the world of new media, however, not only will media be a vehicle for advertising and marketing messages, but it will be *the marketplace itself*. With the convergence of various media—TV, telephone, fax, and the Internet—into a single unified appliance packed with interactive capabilities, commerce will become a two-way street. Instead of having to wait to make your purchases at the appropriate location, you can act immediately. Without leaving your seat, you'll be able to order clothing, groceries, or a car, plan a trip, register for a class, or hire a cleaning service. Trading over the Internet, which is just beginning to take shape, is but a taste of the purchasing power and convenience of new media. With converged media, the opportunities to buy and sell will explode. And you'll trade not via the Internet, but via your new media TV screen.

Of course, no one knows for sure how much buying and selling we'll do through converged media. Some predictions suggest that all of our transactions will happen this way, and that shopping malls will go the way of the dodo. Jeff Bezos, founder of the Internet bookstore Amazon.com suggests that, indeed, "strip malls are history." His own Internet endeavor has critically altered the bookselling and publishing industries. Within four years of its inception in 1995, Amazon.com had driven numerous independent booksellers out of business, and many others were struggling to survive. Like books, music seems to be another natural commodity for Internet trading. The ability to download music from the Internet has already begun affecting the traditional music trade.

While enthusiasm for cybershopping is strong, and investments in Internet trading continue to mount, some analysts take a more moderate approach to the coming revolution. Counterarguments suggest that some things will certainly lend themselves to the interactive buying and selling opportunities of new media, but that traditional retail outlets will remain a necessary part of the marketplace. The truth is, it's too early to tell how much of the public will adopt this new way of buying and selling.

Nonetheless, one thing we don't have to wonder about is whether or not the role of media as a tool for commerce will change. With the convergence of media, its transformation into a virtual marketplace *is* inevitable. Because this marketplace will come right into our homes via a single converged appliance, commerce will be ever-present in our lives, and ever-accessible to our children.

With convergence promising to pump a tidal wave of media options into our households via a single media source, and with technology opening the floodgates to commercial opportunities, we can't help but wonder at the competition that must certainly arise for our attention. As always, media producers and distributors will have to find a way to grab our attention, so that advertisers can get at our wallets. In the age of new media, they'll certainly have their work cut out for them. Of course, they'll rise to the challenge, and we know just how they'll do it: by engaging our emotions through entertainment. Entertainment's power to get our attention and influence our emotions will accelerate in the age of new media. The lines between information, business, advertising, and entertainment are already blurred. With convergence, they'll all but disappear. Entertainment will become more and more of an overwhelming paradigm in the never-ending competition for our attention. Convergent commertainment will be our new way of life.

In greasing the wheels of commerce, media has propelled entertainment to become a dominant experience, indeed a cultural value, in the late twentieth century. Author Michael J. Wolf calls this the *e-factor* (*The Entertainment Economy*, 1999). In the March 1999 issue of *Wired* magazine, Wolf wrote:

So pervasive is the intrusion of entertainment into our daily lives that we have come to look for the e-factor in every aspect of life. We expect that we will be entertained constantly. Products and brands that deliver on this expectation succeed. Products that do not, disappear. Entertainment has, in a way, become the lingua franca of modern commerce, as indispensable as currency.

Advertising has entertainmentized the art of selling: Forget about espousing product attributes; getting us to feel is the key to getting us to buy. As Wolf points out in his book, "there's no business without show business."

Our media-ridden, commerce-driven, entertainment-hungry culture has blurred lines everywhere we look. News is no longer the news of Walter Cronkite's day, when journalism meant delivering information. News today must also entertain in order to keep us watching and ensure network profits. Even education cannot escape the repercussions of our entertainment-oriented society. Faced with the task of reaching a generation of media-grown kids, teachers, in effect, find themselves competing with multimillion-dollar production companies.

More alarming than our societal preoccupation with fun, however, is the effect it's having on our children. While we have come to expect that we will be entertained, our children have learned to *need* this fix. Media is so ingrained in their lives that the e-factor is unavoidable. It has become a way of life, and our children have learned to crave the instant gratification it dishes out. As a result, our educators struggle to teach children with shortened attention spans, decreased curiosity, dulled imaginations, and an inability to work for rewards. We blame these very same teachers for declining reading scores, while ignoring the fact that, before children ever set foot in a classroom, they spend more time watching television than doing any other activity of their waking lives. There's no doubt about it; our present generation of children is wired differently. They expect constant stimulation. "Entertain me" is their mantra; "boring" is the ultimate put-down. For too many of them, a steady diet of media violence has nourished a culture of disrespect. Allowed to feast on helpings of *South Park,* Jerry Springer, professional wrestling, Duke Nukem, and Internet porn sites, "Make my day" has replaced "Have a nice day" as a cultural norm.

When we consider where media is headed, we can hardly shrug off these warning signs. Whereas today we grapple with media in singular dimensions—TV, video games, computers, the Internet—in the era of new media the challenge will be more like 3D. Three inseparable forces—the convergence, commercialization, and entertainmentization of media—will compound to create a media environment that is more pervasive, more engaging, and more powerful. Of course, the potential educational benefits of a multilayered media world are exhilarating. However, media's history reminds us not to bank on noble promises. Media as a business will always come first. Using media to maximize profits will always take precedence over using them to educate a generation of children or build healthy communities. And so, the responsibility for managing media in the lives of children will always belong to parents and caregivers. We will have to meet technology on *our* terms, and learn how to use it appropriately so that our children don't miss out on the advantages it does have to offer. We have no choice but to take this challenge seriously. We don't have the option of saying there's nothing we can do about it. The stakes are just too high. The potential benefits of the new media age are too valuable to be jeopardized by the harm that can be done if we don't get involved. More important, our children are too valuable to give up to media.

• • •

Throughout this book, you have found information, strategies, and tips to help you begin making better media choices in your own home. This is how important change begins. This is why this book was written. Even so, I think we have to believe in something more, as well, in a collective responsibility to establish media-wise families and media-wise communities. We should expect that it is within our power to create families and communities that are aware of the power of media and are motivated to make good media choices. It is our right to demand quality media from those who produce and distribute it. We should envision a world in which the power of media is used to educate our children, to teach attitudes of respect and cooperation, to nurture creativity and imagination. Individually and collectively, we can choose to use media to help us raise a healthier generation of kids, or we can leave it to exploit emotions, make profits, and teach values and attitudes that undermine the health of our society.

Children are the purpose of life. When I think about where media have taken us and where they are going, I always come back to these words. In the face of all that we know about media's power and potential, these words are a wakeup call, a call to action, a reminder of the hope we hold fast in our hearts. It *is* our turn to care. If we take the time to put media where they belong in our families, we can keep them from consuming all the precious space of childhood. If we raise our children to make good media choices for themselves, we fulfill our responsibility to see them safely on their way. And, through it all, we lay the groundwork to carry on this message to the next generation. We have to take our turn to care, as individuals and as a society, so that when the time comes our children can take their turn, too.

Index

About the Authors

David Walsh, Ph.D. is the president and founder of the National Institute on Media and the Family, in Minneapolis. Psychologist, educator, author, and speaker, Dr. Walsh has emerged as one of the leading authorities in America on the impact of media on children and families. His previous books include the award-winning *Selling Out America's Children*. He has spoken to professional and general audiences all over North America, and has been a frequent guest on national radio and television shows. He and his wife, Monica, live with their three children in Minneapolis.

Kristin Parker writes books and video scripts on parenting and children's health. She has recently completed a video project called *Peaceful Parenting,* and is working on a book about parenting in contemporary American society. She lives in Minneapolis with her husband Jeff and three children.

Monica Walsh, M.A., is an educator whose background and experience include the elementary school classroom, special education, parent education, and children's literature. She was a major contributor to the MediaWise parent education program, and has developed curricula for children, teens, and parents.

About the Authors

David Walsh, Ph.D. is the president and founder of the National Institute on Media and the Family, in Minneapolis. Psychologist, educator, author, and speaker, Dr. Walsh has emerged as one of the leading authorities in America on the impact of media on children and families. His previous books include the award-winning *Selling Out America's Children.* He has spoken to professional and general audiences all over North America, and has been a frequent guest on national radio and television shows. He and his wife, Monica, live with their three children in Minneapolis.

Kristin Parker writes books and video scripts on parenting and children's health. She has recently completed a video project called *Peaceful Parenting,* and is working on a book about parenting in contemporary American society. She lives in Minneapolis with her husband Jeff and three children.

Monica Walsh, M.A., is an educator whose background and experience include the elementary school classroom, special education, parent education, and children's literature. She was a major contributor to the MediaWise parent education program, and has developed curricula for children, teens, and parents.